An Economics of
Justice and Charity

AN ECONOMICS

OF

JUSTICE & CHARITY

CATHOLIC SOCIAL TEACHING

ITS DEVELOPMENT AND CONTEMPORARY RELEVANCE

THOMAS STORCK

Foreword by Peter Kwasniewski

Angelico Press

First published in the USA
by Angelico Press 2017
Copyright © Thomas Storck 2017
Foreword © Peter Kwasniewski 2017

For information, address:
Angelico Press, Ltd.
4709 Briar Knoll Dr.
Kettering, OH 45429
www.angelicopress.com

978-1-62138-310-9 pb
978-1-62138-311-6 hb
978-1-62138-309-3 ebook

Book design by
Michael Schrauzer

To the memory of Pope Pius XI,
pontiff of social justice

CONTENTS

Foreword by Peter Kwasniewski   xi

Prefatory Note   xvii

Introduction   1

ONE   From the Beginnings through Leo XIII   9

TWO   From Pius X through Pius XI   19

THREE   From Pius XII through Paul VI   37

FOUR   John Paul II, *Laborem Exercens* and *Sollicitudo Rei Socialis*   49

FIVE   John Paul II, *Centesimus Annus*   63

SIX   Benedict XVI and Francis   81

SEVEN   The Authority of the Church's Social Teaching   97

APPENDIX I   The Question of Usury   105

APPENDIX II   What Does *Centesimus Annus* Really Teach?   131

APPENDIX III   Review of *Compendium of the Social Doctrine of the Church*   143

APPENDIX IV   Is Economic Justice Possible in this World?   149

EPILOGUE   Catholic Social Teaching: Homage to Christ the King   157

About the Author   163

FOREWORD
by Peter Kwasniewski

THE EXCEPTIONALLY USEFUL BOOK YOU ARE HOLDING
in your hands is a historical summary of Catholic social teaching insofar
as that teaching concerns mankind's economic activity. As Thomas Storck
acknowledges, social doctrine extends beyond a concern simply with economic morality and "may be described as that teaching which deals with
the rights and duties of man organized into society"; it finds its ultimate
basis in "the rights of the Creator, Redeemer, and Lord, Christ Himself,
over men and nations," as Pius XI taught in his first encyclical, *Ubi Arcano*.
Nevertheless, ever since Leo XIII's *Rerum Novarum* of 1891, a large part of
the social magisterium of the supreme pontiffs has been directed to the field
of man's economic relations. This is understandable and justified, since it
is in this field that many of the fierce ideological battles of modernity have
been fought. One need only think, for starters, of the intellectual and social
revolutions inspired by Adam Smith, Thomas Malthus, and Karl Marx.

The modern world has been marked by numerous conflicting ideologies,
generally fighting in their own ways against the Catholic faith. Many of these
are well known — socialism, communism, fascism — and few Catholics are
tempted by them. But there is another one that is much more powerful,
more pervasive, more deceiving than any of these: liberalism. Though
American readers may be sure that they know exactly what liberalism is
and why it is an evil, in fact, the term *liberal* in the United States is used
in an unusual manner that partially obscures its true meaning. Liberalism
is nothing other than that generalized revolt against the Church and the
Christian social order that began in the sixteenth century and continues
to this day. Liberalism takes on different forms and champions different
causes, whether of desacralizing political authority, overturning restraints
on economic activity, or, as lately, attacking marriage and the very structure
of human personality.

The Catholic Church has battled relentlessly against liberalism in all its
forms, including economic liberalism, or liberal capitalism, as an attentive

study of Catholic social teaching from Pope Leo XIII to Pope Francis makes clear. In fact, a good case can be made that the central "negative" theme of the modern social magisterium is simply this: liberalism is a disintegrating, destructive force, with no means to heal its self-inflicted wounds and a tendency to provoke extreme reactions that only exacerbate those wounds. Although the Church has reserved her most solemn condemnations for atheistic communism and nationalistic fascism, she has used language no less unambiguous to proscribe the system (not to mention unmask the pretensions) of capitalism as its European inventors understood it, and as their American descendants continue to understand it. In short, there cannot be the slightest doubt that the Church, with her full teaching authority, has excluded both liberal capitalism as well as all varieties of statism or communism as genuine possibilities for a just social order.

Unfortunately, because most Americans cannot conceive of any other possibilities, it is a temptation to think either that the Church has simply condemned everything and thrown up her hands in despair, or that she has, as it were, handed over the messy business of mammon to publicists such as Michael Novak, George Weigel, Thomas Woods, and other American "conservatives" or libertarians who might seem to be more qualified to handle "policy issues." Such publicists tend to posit a tension between the teaching of the popes on economic morality and the supposed findings of economics, or "economic science" as they prefer to term it. But this is a flawed way to proceed. It does not matter what percentage of economists hold this or that position; truth is not arrived at by majority consensus, but by rational discourse anchored in valid first principles. If intelligent objections can be raised against Darwinian evolutionism, when 99.9% of "expert" scientists hold it to be proved beyond doubt as the epitome of "value-free" science, all the more can objections be raised against a discipline to which not a few are unwilling even to extend the honorable name of "science." While economics may be considered as a sort of science, it is one that deals with realities deeply shaped and colored by human freedom — cultural assumptions and expectations, predominant ways of life, government legislation. Basic economic concepts vary from culture to culture depending on many factors; there are no "Platonic ideas" of capital, property, market, wage, price, contract, etc. One may question an excessive confidence in economic dogmas that are far from obviously true, such as the neoclassical view of market price. Indeed, some of the concepts bandied about in mainstream Western economics are fabrications, in both senses of the word: artificial constructs as well as imaginary entities.

Liberal capitalism is a perfect social embodiment of the philosophical liberalism that originated in the salons and parlors of the eighteenth century and became an ever-more dominant feature of European intellectual and political life during the course of the century thereafter. This connection, incidentally, is explicitly made by the popes in their encyclicals; but happily for doubting Thomases, it is also established by secular historical research. What no secular discipline can do or wishes to do, however, is exactly what the popes have unanimously done for over a century: to sound the alarm against this massive intellectual and political aberration, and to condemn its principles as doctrinal and moral errors—and thus, as pertaining to papal competency to pass judgment upon matters of faith and morals. It is therefore an urgent matter for Catholics who wish to be faithful to the teaching Church (*ecclesia docens*) to be aware of her oft-repeated judgment on liberalism. The popes reiterate that economics cannot be rightly understood or virtuously practiced apart from well-ordered politics, culture, and religion: the economic realm is *not* sufficient unto itself or even intelligible in itself, but rather serves as a subordinate element in a complete vision of human life and society, the whole of which must be grasped and assented to before any of its parts can flourish. The health of the part depends on the coherence of the whole.

The papal critique of capitalism is not merely a critique of policies. It is a critique of an ideology, a *Weltanschauung*, a philosophy and way of life, so pervasive in modern Western (or Westernizing) societies and so subtly interwoven into our daily dealings that we fail to notice the poison we are drinking with our milk. The popes of the last century and a half, "watchmen on the walls of Jerusalem" (Is 62:6), have been crying out "Wake up!," their eyes, their brow, betraying immense apprehension as they share in the sufferings of Christ, rejected by His own. How can it be surprising that these few outspoken critics of the modern project are considered by their unbelieving neighbors, or even by their coreligionists, as altogether too extreme in their views, drunk with dreams, driven by an otherworldly piety that lacks a sane counterbalance of worldly know-how?

Given the foregoing, it is obvious that we need, now more than ever, accurate and insightful guides to the Church's social doctrine. This book, like Storck's earlier *From Christendom to Americanism and Beyond*, is just such a guide for our times. Focusing on the specifically *economic* dimension of the papal magisterium, Storck summarizes the chief documents and teachings of the Church's response to the modern social order, as well as various levels of authority that this teaching has and what is binding on Catholic consciences. Right now, too few Catholics are even aware of this wealth of teaching, while at the same time, too many of those who are aware of it create elaborate excuses as to why it has no binding character, or argue that the Church has finally abandoned her opposition to a liberal capitalist social order. The misuse of John Paul II's 1991 encyclical *Centesimus Annus* is a noteworthy example of that ruse; Mr. Storck devotes a chapter and an appendix to explicating the real meaning of that often-misquoted document.

The papal magisterium of the past 150 years offers us a holistic social thinking that is singularly rich and full. Nevertheless, it is no easy task to assimilate it, assent to it, and implement it, particularly in a world ruled by the American capitalist empire, which equips so many with ideological blinders practically from their mothers' wombs (if they survive their mothers' wombs). It is not the least merit of Storck in the present book to lay out clearly and cogently the axioms, arguments, and applications of this social theology as it developed historically. The historical progression in and of itself illustrates how the Holy Spirit, making use of the faith and intellect of pastors and their people, leads the Church into a fuller possession of truth, always in harmony with truth already seen and held. The historical progress of Catholic social thought categorically excludes certain "creative adaptations" or "revisions" that would amount to a repudiation of her Gospel charter and her inflexible commitment to the objective nature of society, the rights of persons created in God's image, and the duties of men and nations to Christ, the King of kings and Lord of lords.

The past century and a half have offered more evidence than we could ever wish for that the health of society, the dignity of persons, and the profession of the true religion stand or fall together. We are living at a time when society is grievously ill, when the poor and the powerless are trampled upon as a matter of course, and when the state of the Church in the Western world is fragmented and crumbling. Yet we cannot stand by indifferently or give way to despair. The world organized by human efforts has collapsed many times as empires rise and fall, but mankind has endured, and more importantly, the Church — beginning, as St. Augustine saw it, with our common father Adam, and embracing every man who follows the divine light — has persevered and will persevere.

An Economics of Justice and Charity bears witness to an important element of that living history of perseverance, wisdom, and evangelization. May it assist Catholics first in learning of the very existence of so rich a body of papal teaching, and then in forming their minds in obedience to the precepts of Christ's Church as these apply to the socio-economic order. *Vivat Christus Rex.*

PREFATORY NOTE

MY AIM IN THIS WORK IS TO GIVE READERS WHO HAVE little or no acquaintance with Catholic social teaching, especially in its modern form, a general overview of the basic documents of that teaching—that is, the chief papal social encyclicals and other documents, as well as the social teachings of the Second Vatican Council. Although Catholic social thought began with the New Testament Church, it is the modern corpus of Catholic social doctrine, which dates from Pope Leo XIII, that people generally mean when they speak of the social teaching of the Church. This body of doctrine is a response to the rise of capitalism, socialism, and industrialism, all of which have introduced new ideas and new ways of living into human affairs. Thus the Church has been forced to take a comprehensive view of man's social relations and to deal with many questions that the patristic or medieval writers never had to consider. The result has been a rich body of social doctrine that sets forth a truly Catholic response to modern conditions. Although a vast secondary literature has come into being expounding and commenting on this doctrine, it is always the teaching of the Magisterium by which all subsidiary writings must be judged. Thus it is always fruitful to return again and again to the sources of the Church's social doctrine and especially to the social encyclicals.

The major part of this book, the first five chapters plus Appendix II, originally appeared as articles in *The Catholic Faith*. Appendix I appeared in *Communio: International Catholic Review*, while Appendices III and IV were originally published in *New Oxford Review*. The epilogue originally appeared as an article in *Catholic Men's Quarterly*. All have been revised to a greater or lesser extent before appearing here in book form. Chapters six and seven were newly written for publication in this volume.

Thomas Storck

INTRODUCTION

AMONG THE TRUTHS TAUGHT BY THE CATHOLIC Church, truths about what we must believe and about how we are to live, are those truths commonly called Catholic social teaching or the Church's social doctrine. They are an important and integral part of Catholic doctrine, but not so well known or so well understood as they might be. I will present this teaching chiefly by way of expounding the principal documents in which it has been articulated by successive popes, as well as by the Second Vatican Council.

Catholic social teaching may be described as that teaching that deals with the rights and duties of men organized into society. Pius XI, one of the most active popes in the field of social doctrine, in his encyclical *Ubi Arcano* (1922), summarized social doctrine as

> Catholic teaching concerning social authority and the due regard for it, concerning the rights and duties of laborers on land or in industry, the relation between the ecclesiastical and the civil power, the rights of the Holy See and the Roman Pontiff, the prerogatives of bishops, and finally the rights of the Creator, Redeemer, and Lord, Christ Himself, over men and nations. (no. 60)

Most often, however, Catholic social teaching is taken in a narrower sense, and refers to the Church's teaching on the morality of the economic aspects of man's life in society — "the rights and duties of laborers on land or in industry" and of the other participants in economic activity, such as property owners. This book, for the most part, will address Catholic social teaching in this latter sense, the Church's teaching on economic morality. But it is important to remember that this teaching on economic morality is connected with and rests upon the Church's teaching on all the points mentioned by Pius XI, particularly the political community.[1]

1 Ever since the New Testament era the Church has addressed questions of her relationship with civil authority, and her doctrine on such matters developed in later centuries as political

Why does the Church involve herself in such secular matters as economics? Is not her only business saving souls? Such questions as these are often raised by Catholics today, with some going so far as to explicitly deny the competence of the Church to deal with matters of economic morality. Others are simply unfamiliar with the reasons for the Church's social doctrine or misunderstand what it is. But in either case, the question deserves full discussion.

First, we should note that the Church's concern with social doctrine is not something new, something that arose only after the Second Vatican Council. Certainly since Vatican II there has been a very unfortunate eclipse of major parts of Catholic doctrine, with sometimes a corresponding emphasis on other parts. In a sense, the transcendent aspects of the faith (those parts that concern God or our future destiny after death) have been de-emphasized by some, and the horizontal aspects (those that concern the community of the faithful) have been emphasized, sometimes even overemphasized. But Catholic social teaching is definitely not a part or product of this latter tendency. The Church's social teaching has its roots in the teachings of Our Lord himself, in the Fathers of the early Church, and in the medieval doctors, such as St. Thomas Aquinas. As Pope Benedict XVI wrote in *Caritas in Veritate*: "Social doctrine is built on the foundation handed on by the Apostles to the Fathers of the Church, and then received and further explored by the great Christian doctors" (no. 12). Its specifically modern presentation began with the pontificate of Leo XIII (1878–1903), especially with the encyclical *Rerum Novarum*, issued in 1891. All of Pope Leo's successors have contributed to the social doctrine of the Church through encyclicals or other documents, and Catholic social teaching was well established long before Vatican II.

Granted that this is the case, why nevertheless did the Church ever embark on this path? The most basic answer to that question is that man, organized in a corporate or social manner—whether into political or civil society, or any entity of a lower order such as a business firm,

---

conditions changed. In response to the modern situation, this teaching was elaborated upon by the nineteenth-century popes, especially Leo XIII in a series of encyclicals including *Diuturnum* (1881), *Immortale Dei* (1885), and *Libertas Praestantissimum* (1888), and Pius XI (in *Quas Primas* (1925). The close connection between Leo XIII's political encyclicals and Catholic economic teaching is mentioned by Pius XI in *Quadragesimo Anno*, no. 2, and by John Paul II in *Centesimus Annus*, no. 4. Likewise, the *Compendium of the Social Doctrine of the Church*, issued by the Pontifical Council for Justice and Peace in 2004, treats of the family and the political community, as well as of the human person.

cooperative, or labor union — is not thereby freed from his duties to Almighty God or to his fellow men. As Pius XI taught in his encyclical *Quas Primas*, "all men, whether collectively or individually, are under the dominion of Christ." For "it would be a grave error...to say that Christ has no authority whatever in civil affairs, since by virtue of the absolute empire over all creatures committed to Him by the Father, all things are in His power."[2] Just because I am a member of society or have cooperated with my neighbor on a project does not exempt me from God's law. Just as human virtue and good works can be regularized or institutionalized in common endeavors (e.g., in a religious order), so also the personal sins of one man can join with the sins of others to result in what St. John Paul II called "structures of sin." Sinful behavior is institutionalized and thus sins "grow stronger, spread, and become the source of other sins, and so influence people's behavior."[3]

This general truth about mankind's cooperation in each other's virtues or vices is likewise true in regard to economic activity. This is because there are many moral questions within the field of economics. A clear and direct statement of this was given by Pope Pius XI in what is perhaps the greatest of the social encyclicals, *Quadragesimo Anno*, issued in 1931. The pontiff wrote:

> We lay down the principle long since clearly established by Leo XIII that it is Our right and Our duty to deal authoritatively with social and economic problems. It is not of course for the Church to lead men to transient and perishable happiness only, but to that which is eternal. Indeed "the Church believes that it would be wrong for her to interfere without just cause in such earthly concerns"; but she never can relinquish her God-given task of interposing her authority, not indeed in technical matters, for which she has neither the equipment nor the mission, but in all those that have a bearing on moral conduct. For the deposit of truth entrusted to Us by God, and Our weighty office of propagating, interpreting and urging in season and out of season the entire moral law, demand that both social and economic questions be brought within Our supreme jurisdiction, in so far as they refer to moral issues. (no. 41)

---

2 Encyclical *Quas Primas*, nos. 17–18.

3 Encyclical *Sollicitudo Rei Socialis*, no. 36. The concept of "structures of sin" is taken here from the apostolic exhortation *Reconciliatio et Paenitentia* (December 2, 1984).

> For, though economic activity and moral discipline are guided
> each by its own principles in its own sphere, it is false that the two
> orders are so distinct and alien that the former in no way depends
> on the latter. (no. 42)

What can be learned from this teaching of Pius XI? First, it is obvious
that those who teach that economics is a self-contained discipline in no
way subject to ethics or moral theology are simply wrong. We will see
in our discussion of the more than one hundred years of modern social
teaching what the Church has taught and why she has taught it. But at
the outset we should remember that the Church and the moral order
undoubtedly have an important function in economic affairs. Moreover,
it is for the Church, not for economists, to pronounce the roles and limits
of ethics and theology in economics.

Second, we can see that, as Pope John Paul II put it, the Church's social
teaching "belongs to the field... of *theology* and particularly of moral
theology."[4] In other words, the Church is interested in social and economic matters only in so far as they are really moral issues. The Church
would not, for example, propose the best way of dealing with inflation nor
teach us exactly what rate of taxation would raise the most revenue. But
where the economy touches on moral questions, that is another matter.
And since the economy concerns matters of property, contracts, wages,
work, and many other dealings of man with man, obviously it includes
many moral questions that must be brought under the twin virtues of
justice and charity. Thus the popes have looked at social matters neither
as economists nor as politicians, but rather as pastors with both the moral
and the physical — and indeed the eternal — welfare of mankind at heart.

No part of Catholic teaching can really be separated from the rest,
and of course this holds true for social doctrine as well. In the secular
political and social discourse that takes place in our time, people make
many statements about rights and duties, but for the most part these
statements are grounded in nothing. That is, almost no one seems to
think it is necessary to show how his political and social opinions can be
derived from the nature of man or the nature of society. Yet how can we
talk about man's rights and duties unless we first know exactly what man
is? Is he simply a complex machine or perhaps a complicated animal, but

---

4 *Sollicitudo Rei Socialis*, no. 41.

not different in kind from the brute beasts? Many people today assume one or the other of these views, yet at the same time they illogically posit all sorts of rights and duties for men. But it is hard to see how machines could have rights or apes duties. The Church, however, is different. She elaborates a view of man based on both Holy Scripture and Sacred Tradition as well as reason, and from this view draws the necessary corollaries about man's life in society. Thus, as St. John XXIII explained in *Mater et Magistra*, "the social teaching proclaimed by the Catholic Church cannot be separated from her traditional teaching regarding man's life" (no. 222). And therefore the "teaching and spreading of her social doctrine are part of the Church's evangelizing mission."[5]

This is simply another aspect of the fact that Catholicism is not an individualistic religion. In the first letter to the Corinthians, chapter 12, St. Paul describes the Church as the Mystical Body of Jesus Christ. He speaks of the various functions or apostolates in the Church, each of which is given "for the common good." He compares the Church to a human body, each part of which needs the others. And he sums up his teaching by saying: "If one member suffers, all suffer together; if one member is honored, all rejoice together." This doctrine is the foundation for much that we take for granted in our Catholic life; for example, the intercession of the saints for us, or our intercession and gaining of indulgences for those in purgatory. As Catholics, we are linked in innumerable ways with our brethren, both in and beyond time. But as Holy Scripture in many places makes clear, we are brothers not just to our fellow Catholics, but to all people. "So then, as we have opportunity, let us do good to all men, and especially to those who are of the household of faith" (Galatians 6:10). Catholic social teaching, then, is founded on both the natural and supernatural bonds that unite the whole human race, and thus, as an integral part of the Gospel, is connected to some of the most central truths of the faith.

I would have to be a hermit, however, not to realize that often interpretation of Catholic social teaching is a controversial matter. Of course it is legitimate to discuss precisely what is meant by this or that papal statement, or how exactly we may implement something, or even whether a certain papal suggestion might not necessarily be appropriate for all times or places. But debates on the Church's social doctrine often go far beyond this. They often assume aspects of the partisan conflicts that occur in the

---

5 *Sollicitudo Rei Socialis*, no. 41.

secular world over economic and social policy. Sometimes it seems as if those who use papal teaching to support positions they already hold are more numerous than those who are willing to sit down and learn with a docile heart what God's Church is proposing for our belief and conduct.

The chief reason for this, I think, is that most come to the Church's teaching with previously formed and strongly held opinions on socio-economic matters. Most of us are raised and formed in a milieu in which we receive what we call either liberal or conservative ideas.[6] Therefore, when we come upon statements from the Church's Magisterium dealing with economic questions, there is a human tendency to look for those statements that tend to support what we already believe and to overlook or explain away those that do not. And perhaps most egregiously, there is a tendency to *interpret* these statements in the context of one or another secular political philosophy. That is, instead of seeing all Catholic social teaching as a consistent whole, from which we are to learn, many take statements that have a superficial similarity to either liberal or conservative principles and interpret them as part of one or the other of those secular ideologies. As Fr. John Cronin wrote:

> If [someone] combs through [the social encyclicals], only taking passages that seem to support his position and ignoring those that appear to contradict his thinking, then his approach is wrong. He is not seeking to learn. He is merely using the popes, and misusing their teaching, to confirm his preconceptions.[7]

Catholic social doctrine is neither liberal nor conservative. Neither is it correct to say that it is partly liberal and partly conservative. It has a logic of its own which, when we grasp it, allows us to see not only that both liberalism and conservatism offer only partial truths and partial solutions, but also that the basic approach of each is erroneous. If we hope to form our intellects according to the mind of the Church on socio-economic questions, then we must discard both conservative and liberal perspectives in order to learn how to think with the Church.

---

6 I am using the terms *liberal* and *conservative* according to their current American usage, but elsewhere in this book the term liberal and its derivatives will be used in the sense they bear in Church documents. See p. 33, note 3 for a discussion of this point.

7 John F. Cronin, *Christianity and Social Progress: A Commentary on* Mater et Magistra (Baltimore: Helicon, 1965), 20–21.

Granted, it is difficult to give up or modify our views on social and economic questions because of Church doctrine. But the mark of an orthodox Catholic must be a ready submission to the Magisterium's authentic teaching. Catholics must be as prepared to yield to the judgment of the Church in social matters as they are in other matters. And the mere fact that others — those who are regarded as political enemies — may misuse Catholic social teaching does not give anyone the right to do the same. If we approach Catholic doctrine in this manner we will get nowhere. As far as possible, as we study social doctrine, we must try to forget the bitter controversies raging in the secular political world. For we are studying theology, not economics or politics. This is not to say, of course, that social doctrine has no application in the real world. It certainly does. But we must still approach it in the spirit of children of the Gospel and the Church, not as if we were debaters preparing our briefs.

Some Catholics have raised objections to the pastoral statements from bishops and bishops' conferences concerned with social doctrine. I will not deal with them in this book, but only with papal teaching and the teaching of the Second Vatican Council. To the extent that the teaching of bishops simply repeats papal teaching, it is already contained in the latter. Pastoral statements that do not simply repeat papal teachings can be an attempt to apply those teachings to the specific conditions of one nation or region. This is a necessary task, but not one I will be discussing here, for such teaching does not enjoy the same divine guidance as does that of the popes.

One persistent criticism of Catholic social teaching is that, however well-intentioned it might be, it is impractical and could never be put into effect. The best reply to such a criticism is to look closely at this teaching and see exactly what it calls for, and whether and how it could be applied in this world. This we will do, in part, in the subsequent chapters in this book. But we can make some general observations about this now. First, we should ask ourselves the questions: Can the Ten Commandments be implemented in the real world? Are they practical teachings for today? Any true Catholic knows that they are, but at the same time realizes that, unfortunately, they are not being put into effect by most of the human race. They could be, but they are not. That is to say, with the help of God, each one of us could live, albeit imperfectly, by all of God's commandments. The same can be said of Catholic social teaching. With the help of God and under the guidance of the Church, mankind could indeed

live, again imperfectly, in a way more pleasing to God. The injustices that
the popes have spoken against could in great part be eliminated. Social
charity could be the cement that holds society together. But, like the Ten
Commandments, this requires first that we turn to God and truly seek
His assistance. If we do this, then Catholic social teaching would not be
beyond the reach of human beings.[8]

If we keep these reflections in mind while studying social doctrine, we
can avoid seeing in the Church's teaching only reinforcements of our own
ideologies. As I said, this is a fundamental distortion of social doctrine. In
the first chapter, I will be dealing with the roots of Catholic social teaching in Sacred Scripture and its development up through Pope Leo XIII,
especially with his great encyclical, *Rerum Novarum* of 1891, in which we
can see both a summation of all the Church taught on the social question
since the time of Our Lord, as well as a foundation for all that has followed.

✳ ✳ ✳

Quotations from encyclicals in this book are from various sources. Scrip-
tural references are from the Revised Standard Version, Catholic Edition.
Generally, the encyclicals of Leo XIII, Pius XI, John XXIII, and Paul VI
are from *Seven Great Encyclicals* (Paulist Press, 1963). References to and
quotations from the apostolic letter *Octogesima Adveniens* of Paul VI and
the encyclicals of John Paul II and Francis are from the editions published
by the Daughters of St. Paul, while quotations from Benedict XVI's writings
are as published by the United States Conference of Catholic Bishops. In
all cases, the paragraph numbers conform to the numbering used on the
Vatican website, where the full text of each encyclical may be found under
the respective pontiff. Slight alterations in capitalization in the texts have
been made for clarity or to reflect contemporary usage.

---

8 This point is discussed at length in Appendix III.

ONE

From the Beginnings
through Leo XIII

THE SOCIAL APOSTOLATE OF THE CHURCH BEGAN
while her founder, Jesus Christ, was still on this earth. In fact,
even before the Incarnation, during the dispensation of the Old
Covenant, the law of God and his prophets insisted continually on justice
and on charity toward the poor. For example, the law of Moses proclaims
that every seventh year "every creditor shall release what he has lent to
his neighbor" (Deuteronomy 15:2), and nearly every prophet denounces
those "who oppress the poor, who crush the needy" (Amos 4:2). Social
justice was linked with faithfulness to the God of Israel and the keeping
of his covenant.

This continues in the New Testament. During Our Lord's ministry,
he made it clear on more than one occasion that if those who were to
become members of his Mystical Body did not fulfill their duties toward
their neighbors—both of justice and of charity—then their faith was
in vain and they could not expect an eternal reward. The parable of the
sheep and the goats in Matthew 25:31–46, for example, presents the issue
of salvation or damnation as resting solely on how we treat the poor: the
hungry and thirsty, strangers, the naked, the sick, prisoners. The Apostle
Paul tells us that "those who desire to be rich fall into temptation, into a
snare, into many senseless and hurtful desires that plunge men into ruin
and destruction" (2 Timothy 5:9). And St. James warns the rich: "Come
now, you rich, weep and howl for the miseries that are coming upon you"
(James 5:1). Altogether, the witness of both Old and New Testaments
insists on the duties of justice and charity by both individuals and the
community toward the poor.

After the Apostolic Age, this tradition of teaching on justice and charity
was continued by the Fathers of the Church, the theologians and saints of

the Church's early centuries who shaped so much of the doctrine, liturgy, and ascetical practice of Catholicism. Many of them used quite striking language to insist on our duties to our neighbor—as in St. John Chrysostom's statement: "Not to enable the poor to share in our goods is to steal from them and deprive them of life. The goods we possess are not ours, but theirs."[1]

In the Middle Ages, as a well-developed Christian society came into being, the scholastic doctors, such as St. Thomas Aquinas, had the leisure to survey the entire field of the virtues, including justice and charity, and to comment on the duties of rulers and subjects and the right organization of the state and society. As a result, building on both reason and revelation, they developed the implications of the Fathers' teaching regarding the just price, the illicitness of usury, and, in general, the idea that economic affairs are subject to the moral law; the plea of economic utility or necessity could not override the commandments of God.

Toward the end of the Middle Ages economic life in Europe changed rapidly. Capitalism—that is, the separation of ownership and work— became widely established, the almost wholly agricultural life of previous centuries declined, and commercial and even industrial ventures became more common and more economically important. In the newly Protestant regions of Europe, the novel doctrines that were preached by Luther, Calvin, and their associates and successors quickly became a major stimulus for engaging in economic activity purely for the sake of gain, divorced from its social context. But many parts of Catholic Europe experienced major economic changes as well. Merchants, for example, increasingly resented the prohibition against usury, and in an effort to evade the canonical penalties, introduced new forms of contracts that disguised the probable existence of usury under complicated legal formulas.[2] Catholic theologians and moralists examined these new phenomena with some care, seeking where possible to harmonize them with the moral law. There was considerable difference of opinion about some points, and in general, the Church did not issue a clarion call to reconstruct the changing economic life of society according to the Gospel. In part this was because by the eighteenth century most of the ruling elites of Catholic countries were Catholic in name only, and not much interested in Christian living, either on a personal or societal level.

---

1 St. John Chrysostom, *Hom. in Lazaro* 2, 5: PG 48, 992.
2 For example, what was known as the triple contract or *contractus trinus*. For a full account of these developments, see Appendix I.

Beginning with the French revolution of 1789, and the quarter century of wars that followed, the entire public basis of society in Catholic Europe began to change. As the nineteenth century progressed, no longer did most governments pretend that the public life of their nations was entirely shaped by Catholic faith and morals. Now a fierce clash of ideologies became the rule for Western civilization. Each of these various ideologies, from Marxism to laissez-faire capitalism, held itself out as the final answer. Into the midst of this clash of ideologies came Pope Leo XIII, determined to revive the best of Christian civilization, so that a distinctively Catholic voice would be heard, in order to rally the faithful, attract men of good will to the Church, and try to rebuild a Christian social order.

When Leo came to the throne of Peter in 1878 he found the Church in a discouraged state. Despite the real successes of the First Vatican Council in 1870, shortly thereafter the kingdom of Italy overran what remained of the Papal States, ending the Council prematurely and depriving Pope Pius IX of his civil sovereignty. Everywhere in Europe, Catholic political causes seemed to be losing, while what remained of the old Christian social order was rapidly passing away. Leo XIII restored the confidence of the Catholic world and began to reinvigorate the Church with an energy that lasted until the early 1960s. He did this chiefly by showing how the crisis of modern times could be met by drawing on and elaborating on elements already present in Catholic faith and tradition.

Leo and his successors were very successful in creating a distinctively Catholic response to the modern world. The Catholic intellectual revival, which had begun even before Leo's pontificate, grew stronger, attracted many converts to the Church, and gave Catholics a confidence that the faith really contained the solution for all the modern problems of individuals, families, and societies. Leo realized that the challenges presented by the new philosophies had to be met by a thorough intellectual analysis, not only of the nature of man and of society, but also of human thought itself. In one of his earliest encyclicals, *Aeterni Patris* of 1879, he called for the renewed study of scholastic philosophy and theology, especially that of St. Thomas Aquinas, so the Church would be equipped to address the questions raised by the new thinkers on their own level. In addition, he wrote a series of encyclicals addressing the political and social problems raised by the society that had come into being since 1789, a society largely without any religious basis. Leo did not compromise with what was anti-Christian in the new order. Instead he showed how what was perennial in the Church's teaching could be made the foundation for a renewed modern society.

In the past, although the rich often exploited the poor, every Christian society was officially committed to justice and a sufficiency for each person. However little it may have lived up to it, Christendom upheld the ideal of society as a family. As the historian Christopher Dawson wrote of the Middle Ages: "Every individual and every corporation [guild] had their special offices to fulfill in the Commonwealth, and each was entitled to a just reward."[3] But this was no longer the case in the nineteenth century. Some thinkers, such as Marx, openly advocated class warfare; others, such as adherents of the Manchester school of economists in England, taught that the problems of the poor were of no concern to others and that it was wrong for the state or any private person to intervene on behalf of workers, who, by a dictate of nature, were forever doomed to poverty at starvation wages. Meanwhile, industrialization had reduced the poor to a state worse than ever: "little better than slavery," as Leo XIII was to write.[4]

Into this welter of opinions Pope Leo brought the first modern social encyclical to focus specifically on economic questions, *Rerum Novarum* of 1891. He himself, in the opening section of the encyclical, speaks of the changes that had overcome the economic order, "the growth of industry, and the surprising discoveries of science; the changed relations of masters and workmen; the enormous fortunes of individuals and the poverty of the masses..." (no. 1). Leo then gives his analysis of the root causes of the situation of his day.

> But all agree, and there can be no question whatever, that some remedy must be found, and found quickly, for the misery and wretchedness which press so heavily at this moment on the large majority of the very poor. The ancient workmen's Guilds were destroyed in the last century, and no other organization took their place. Public institutions and the laws have repudiated the ancient religion. Hence by degrees it has come to pass that working men have been given over, isolated and defenseless, to the callousness of employers and the greed of unrestrained competition. (no. 3)

3 "Catholicism and Economics, Part III. The Economic Problem of the Present Age," *New Blackfriars*, 5, no. 52 (1924): 210–19.

4 *Rerum Novarum*, no. 3.

Here is a statement of the economic situation as it existed in the late nineteenth century. What was the pontiff's response? What could the Church recommend as an aid to the poor?

The first point Leo makes is that the institution of private property, then under fierce attack from socialists, could not rightly be abolished, and that private property, far from hurting the poor, in fact helped them—at least potentially. Since this point is so important, it deserves some attention.

Leo is not shy about admitting that in his day property was not well distributed. As a result, the rich were able to oppress the poor with impunity.

> On the one side there is the party which holds the power because it holds the wealth; which has in its grasp all labor and all trade; which manipulates for its own benefit and its own purposes all the sources of supply, and which is powerfully represented in the councils of the State itself. On the other side there is the needy and powerless multitude, sore and suffering, always ready for disturbance. (no. 47)

Faced with these facts, the socialists indicted the very system of private property. If only the state controlled the goods of the world, they argued, "each citizen will then have his equal share of whatever there is to enjoy" (no. 4). But Leo showed how foolish that doctrine was, and that, were it instituted, "the working man himself would be among the first to suffer" (ibid.). But in saying this he was by no means upholding the present system as such. Instead, like the philosopher he was, Leo grounds the institution of private property in human nature itself, not in mere custom or convention. Pope Leo shows from reason that, since man is endowed with an intellect and is able to foresee his future needs, he must be able to provide against those future needs by his own industry. And for this he obviously requires things "in stable and permanent possession; he must have not only things which perish in the using, but also those which, though used, remain for use in the future" (no. 6). A man, for example, can more easily provide his food by having his own land on which to grow it, than by wandering through the uncultivated forest looking for wild edible plants.

Most importantly, among the various points in favor of the private ownership of property that Leo XIII brings forward, he points out the benefits of private property for the head of each family.

> That right of property, therefore, which has been proved to belong
> naturally to individual persons must also belong to a man in his
> capacity of head of a family; nay, such a person must possess this
> right so much the more clearly in proportion as his position multi-
> plies his duties. (no. 13)

If this is the case, and if property is to sustain the poor as much as the
rich, how are the poor to acquire property? How can a more just distribution of property be effected? A working man has only one source of
income — the wages of his labor. And therefore, Leo XIII is quite explicit
that a working man's wages ought to be sufficient for him and his family not only to live "in reasonable comfort," but also "by cutting down
expenses, to put by a little property" (no. 46). However, if a worker is to
purchase property, obviously his wages must be sufficient to permit him
to save. Thus we must look at another major theme of this encyclical, the
question of wages and their justice.

The pope is quite forthright about Catholic teaching on this issue. He
mentions the prevailing secular notion that wages

> are fixed by free consent; and, therefore, the employer when he pays
> what was agreed upon has done his part, and is not called upon for
> anything further. The only way, it is said, in which injustice could
> happen, would be if the master refused to pay the whole of the wages,
> or the workman would not complete the work undertaken; when
> this happens the State should intervene, to see that each obtains his
> own, but not under any other circumstances. (no. 43)

Leo's answer to this is firm: "This mode of reasoning is by no means
convincing to a fair-minded man, for there are important considerations
which it leaves out of view altogether" (no. 44). Because a man without
property *must* work, "it follows that each one has a right to procure what
is required in order to live; and the poor can procure it in no other way
than by work and wages" (ibid.). In other words, if a man's wages are
fixed too low to support himself or his family by his day's work, what is
he supposed to do? Work all night, too? Send his wife and children to
work? Any worker who is forced to accept too low wages "because an
employer or contractor will give him no better…is the victim of force and
injustice" (no. 45). Although *Rerum Novarum* was written over a century

ago, these words should still have a bite for us today, since by no means is the concept of a living wage universally accepted, and more than a few workers are victims "of force and injustice" in this manner.

Whose task is it to see that workers' wages are sufficient? Is it the task of the government, through a central bureaucracy or minimum wage laws? Pope Leo does not rule out such an approach, but his clear preference is for another method. In doing so, he brings to the fore one of the most interesting proposals (at the same time both traditional and innovative) in the entire corpus of Catholic social teaching. This is the notion of self-regulation by mutual agreement between workers and employers.

The necessary background to this proposal is found earlier in the encyclical, where Leo points out the following truth:

> The great mistake that is made in the matter now under consideration, is to possess oneself of the idea that class is naturally hostile to class; that rich and poor are intended by nature to live at war with one another. So irrational and so false is this view, that the exact contrary is the truth. Just as the symmetry of the human body is the result of the disposition of the members of the body, so in a State it is ordained by nature that these two classes should exist in harmony and agreement, and should, as it were, fit into one another, so as to maintain the equilibrium of the body politic. Each requires the other; capital cannot do without labor nor labor without capital. Mutual agreement results in pleasantness and good order; perpetual conflict necessarily produces confusion and outrage. (no. 19)

This insight from the Church is opposed to socialism with its notions of inevitable class conflict, but in many respects it is also opposed to our own system. For implicit in our economic arrangements is the idea that owners and employers make money by cutting the wages of employees or moving jobs overseas to cheaper locales. These practices naturally pit one side against the other. But this need not be. Leo adumbrates here, but later Pius XI will say the same thing with much more detail: if both sides in the labor conflict will submit themselves to justice, then harmony can result because each side will be submitting to a higher standard. Neither side will triumph over the other; rather both sides will accept fully their duties as well as their rights.

After explaining that workers and employers are not naturally hostile to each other, Leo then brings forth the notion of "societies or boards" (no. 45), which he suggests would do a better job of addressing the questions of wages, hours of work, and safety and health conditions in the workplace than a state bureaucracy would. What is Pope Leo talking about here? He is setting forth the idea of joint committees or societies of workmen and employers or owners, who together will address their common problems. Forty years later, Pope Pius XI will elaborate on this idea in the encyclical *Quadragesimo Anno*. But here Leo XIII gives only an outline of such a society's workings and functions.

The pontiff sees the need for organization and joint action on the part of workers, since individually they are helpless before the power of their employers. In this sense, labor unions would fall into this category. So also would mutual insurance societies for workingmen and their families. But Leo hoped that societies could be formed that would overcome the sharp employer/employee division, in the sense that hostility and confrontation would be replaced by good will and justice. If these groups could be successful in improving working conditions and wages, and lessening strife between owners and workers, then the need for direct state action would be removed, or at least reduced. The pope notes that many of the existing labor organizations of his time were socialistic in their principles and hostile to the Church. Naturally he wishes that, whenever possible, Catholics be formed into Catholic organizations, where not only the economic, but also the spiritual needs of the workers could be met.

One other major theme of *Rerum Novarum* needs mention in order to complete Leo XIII's teaching. This is his insistence on the *duty* of the rich to give liberally of their possessions to the poor. He quotes St. Thomas Aquinas: "Man should not consider his outward possessions as his own, but as common to all, so as to share them without difficulty when others are in need" (no. 22). Although, as Leo notes, this duty is not usually enforced in courts of law, it will nevertheless be enforced by the last Judge whom we shall all meet.

> Therefore, those whom fortune favors are warned that freedom from
> sorrow and abundance of earthly riches are no guarantee of that
> beatitude that shall never end, but rather of the contrary; that the
> rich should tremble at the threatenings of Jesus Christ — threatenings

so strange in the mouth of our Lord; and that a most strict account
must be given to the Supreme Judge for all that we possess. (ibid.)

Later, Pius XI will point out how necessary this social charity is, joined to
social justice, to bring about a true Christian social order.

Leo XIII was so successful in *Rerum Novarum* because he drew on
the entire existing corpus of Catholic social thought. And therefore later
popes, including John Paul II, have been able in turn to draw on *Rerum
Novarum*, stressing and elaborating on certain themes, but showing how
that brilliant document is never out of date. As we progress through the
body of papal social teaching, again and again we will see *Rerum Novarum*
cited, applied, and developed as the Church's social doctrine grew to meet
the changing needs of the world.

TWO

From Pius X
through Pius XI

IN THE LAST CHAPTER I SPOKE OF LEO XIII, AND ESPE-
cially of his great encyclical *Rerum Novarum* of 1891. Leo XIII was the
first pope to systematically evaluate modern economic conditions in
the light of the teaching of the Church, and the tradition he began has
continued and developed to this day. In the current chapter, I will cover
the period from the reign of St. Pius X (1903 to 1914) to the death of Pius
XI (1939). During this time successive popes developed the doctrine of
Rerum Novarum according to the needs of the time, in particular in the
encyclical Pius XI issued in 1931 to commemorate its fortieth anniversary.

Pius X, the successor of Leo XIII, did not issue any general social
encyclical, but his activities in regard to social issues are still noteworthy.
Long before his elevation to the papacy, while still a parish priest, he took
a lively interest in both the spiritual and temporal needs of his flock and
helped to found cooperative banks or credit unions so that his parish-
ioners would have a safe place for their money and access to credit without
having to resort to usurers. In his letter of 1910 to the bishops of France,
Notre Charge Apostolique, he condemned a sincere but misguided French
social movement called Le Sillon. St. Pius exhorted the bishops to "take
an active part in the organization of society" so that "all men of good will"
may "attain their legitimate share of temporal happiness." And in his 1912
encyclical to the German bishops, *Singulari Quadam*, he restated Leo's
support of labor unions, especially Catholic unions, but also labor unions
of mixed religion where such were necessary.

Pius's successor, Benedict XV (1914–1922), reigned during the First
World War, and was occupied chiefly with the war and its aftermath. He
greatly assisted refugees and others threatened with starvation by the war,
but did not issue a social encyclical.

Next elected was Pius XI (1922–1939), in my opinion one of the greatest popes of the twentieth century and who did more to develop the Church's social doctrine than possibly any other pontiff. His encyclicals cover many subjects including the kingship of Jesus Christ, Christian marriage, Christian education, and communism. In his 1925 encyclical *Quas Primas*, he made clear the fact that Jesus Christ is king of both individuals and nations, and introduced the Feast of Christ the King into the Church's calendar and liturgy. In the 1931 encyclical *Casti Connubii*, he was the first pope to solemnly condemn birth control. He was very active in the social apostolate; in many ways his chief social encyclical, *Quadragesimo Anno* of 1931, remains the major source for all subsequent papal social teachings.[1] His 1937 encyclical, *Divini Redemptoris*, directed against communism, is at the same time a critique of the economies of the capitalist nations, and repeats and develops some of the proposals previously made in *Quadragesimo Anno*.

So clearly did Pius XI realize that the Church's social doctrine was an integral part of the Gospel, that he touched on such matters even in his encyclical on Christian marriage. Toward the end of that encyclical, after pointing out the temporal needs of large families and poor families, the pontiff wrote:

> Wherefore, those who have the care of the State and of the public good cannot neglect the needs of married people and their families, without bringing great harm upon the State and on the common welfare. Hence, in making the laws and in disposing of public funds they must do their utmost to relieve the needs of the poor, considering such a task as one of the most important of their administrative duties. (no. 121)

Leo XIII had recognized that at times the state authorities would have to act directly on behalf of justice and charity, but here as elsewhere, Pius XI develops Leo's teaching by making more explicit what was often only implicit in *Rerum Novarum*.

Pius's greatest achievement in the social field, however, was *Quadragesimo Anno*, issued on the precise day, May 15, forty years after *Rerum*

---

1 This is not to say that it supplants *Rerum Novarum* in importance, but rather that it develops the teaching of *Rerum Novarum* so well and so fully that there are scarcely any concrete proposals made by later popes that were not first made or suggested in *Quadragesimo Anno*.

Novarum. So ambitious was the pope's goal in this encyclical, that in truth, the Catholic world has not yet assimilated, let alone implemented, its teaching. Though papal encyclicals are usually known by their opening Latin words, each encyclical also has a formal title. The title of *Quadragesimo Anno* reads in part, *On Reconstructing the Social Order and Perfecting It Conformably to the Precepts of the Gospel.* Such a reconstruction of the entire social order is obviously a gigantic task, and it is not surprising that Catholics have often shrunk from the hard work that would be required. As we look at the contents of this encyclical, we will better see what is entailed in such an undertaking.

Since the occasion of *Quadragesimo Anno* was to commemorate the fortieth anniversary of *Rerum Novarum,* Pius XI devotes the first part to giving some of the background of Leo's encyclical and explaining the benefits that have resulted from it. He reminds his readers of the harsh conditions that the workers, "oppressed by dire poverty," experienced toward the end of the nineteenth century. Leo's teaching gave new hope to workers, "who felt themselves vindicated and defended by the highest authority on earth" (no. 13). Moreover, after the encyclical's issuance, Catholics, both clerics and laymen — and even some non-Catholics — began to promote and implement its teaching in various ways. For example, before *Rerum Novarum,* most rulers and governments felt that they must restrict themselves to being "mere guardians of law and order." Pius goes on to comment:

> We do not, of course, deny that even before the Encyclical of Leo, some rulers had provided for the more urgent needs of the working classes, and had checked the more flagrant acts of injustice perpetrated against them. But after the Apostolic Voice had sounded from the Chair of Peter throughout the world, the leaders of the nations, at last more conscious of their obligations, set their hearts and minds to the promotion of a broader social policy. (no. 26)

Moreover, "not a few recent laws dealing with social questions were originally proposed to the suffrages of the people's representatives by ecclesiastics thoroughly imbued with Leo's teaching" (no. 27). As a result there grew up "a new branch of jurisprudence," to safeguard "the soul, the health, the strength, the housing, workshops, wages, dangerous employments, in a word, all that concerns the wage earners, with particular regard to women and children" (no. 28).

Next Pope Pius takes up the question of labor unions, and points out that in the nineteenth century governments often

> regarded...unions of workingmen with disfavor, if not with open hostility. While readily recognizing and protecting similar associations among other classes, with shameful hurt they denied the innate right of forming associations to those who needed them most for self-protection against oppression by the more powerful. (no. 30)

But again, *Rerum Novarum* helped to change this.

> It must be set to the credit of the Encyclical that these unions of workingmen have everywhere so flourished, that in our days, though unfortunately still inferior in number to the organizations of socialists and communists, they already muster an imposing body of wage earners able to maintain successfully, both in national and international assemblies, the rights and legitimate demands of Catholic laborers, and to assert the saving principle on which Christian society is based. (no. 36)

Even from this first part of *Quadragesimo Anno*, one can learn something of Pius's teaching on social and economic matters. Although the necessity for some state intervention in economic matters and the positive role of unions are mentioned in *Rerum Novarum*, Pius discusses them more explicitly. This is a legitimate development of doctrine, denying nothing that was authoritatively said in the past, but responding to new questions and conditions, bringing out the implications of earlier teaching or applying it in new ways.

After this introduction, Pius proceeds to the second part of *Quadragesimo Anno*, in which he will "develop as regards certain points the teaching of so great a master on social and economic affairs, after vindicating it from some doubts which have arisen." He begins this part by reasserting the authority of the Church, and especially of the sovereign pontiff "to deal authoritatively with social and economic problems" (no. 41). His statement here ought to be sufficient to silence those who claim that popes have no business speaking about such matters. Those who make such claims are wrong, not because the Church has authority in "technical matters," but because many economic questions are really moral questions or are intimately related to moral questions. I discussed this point at length in the introduction.

First, Pius XI takes up the question of property. He, of course, upholds the institution of private property, but he also expands several points made earlier by Leo XIII. He notes that different societies have had different concepts of property, and while the government has no right to abolish private property, nevertheless because property has a social as well as an individual character, there is a role for the state in making clearer the social duties of property owners (no. 46). He says:

> However, when civil authority adjusts ownership to meet the needs of the public good it acts not as an enemy, but as the friend of private owners; for thus it effectively prevents the possession of private property, intended by Nature's Author in His Wisdom for the sustaining of human life, from creating intolerable burdens and so rushing to its own destruction. It does not therefore abolish but protects private ownership, and far from weakening the right of private property, it gives it new strength. (no. 49)

One can see from this that the Church does not teach a right to private property that is absolute. Property ownership has duties toward the common good and is subject to limits. Although Pius XI does not mention them, zoning laws would be one example of laws that, as he puts it, "specify... what is licit and what is illicit for property owners" (no. 49).

After this, the pontiff discusses wages. Leo XIII had devoted a large section of *Rerum Novarum* to wages, and had taught that they must be sufficient to support the wage earner and his family "in reasonable and frugal comfort." Pius XI reaffirms this teaching (no. 71), but he goes further and says that in the past too much of the profits of business and industry had accrued to the rich: "Capital...claimed all the...profits and left to the laborer the barest minimum..." (no. 54). "Every effort, therefore, must be made that at least in future only a fair share of the fruits of production be permitted to accumulate in the hands of the wealthy, and that an ample sufficiency be supplied to the workingmen" (no. 61).

In connection with the question of wages, Pius XI uses the term *social justice*, a term that he had himself introduced into the corpus of Catholic teaching in his 1923 encyclical *Studiorum Ducem*. Speaking of situations in which the state of economic life does not allow "fathers of families [to]

receive a sufficient wage adequate to meet ordinary domestic needs," Pius
states that "social justice demands that reforms be introduced without
delay which will guarantee every adult workingman just such a wage"
(no. 71). In other words, social justice is the virtue that commands those
involved in the political and economic orders to restructure society, if
necessary, so that wage justice can be achieved. Social justice concerns our
duty toward society as a whole. We will see this point developed further
in Pius's encyclical *Divini Redemptoris*.

The next topic that Pius XI takes up is the immense one stated in the
title of the encyclical, the reconstruction of the social order. This reconstruction is divided into two essential parts, "the reform of institutions
and the correction of morals." Pius treats moral reform in the third and
last section of the encyclical, and turns his attention first to the reform
of institutions. This is probably the most important section of *Quadragesimo Anno*, for in it Pius XI elaborates his teaching about "occupational
groups," sometimes known in the United States as "industry councils,"
or perhaps more familiarly, as guilds. But first he introduces the concept
of subsidiarity and begins the discussion by reminding his readers about
that "highly developed social life which once flourished in a variety of
prosperous and interdependent institutions," but which has subsequently
been destroyed "leaving virtually only individuals and the State..." (no. 78).
What is the pope speaking about? In the English-speaking world we are
apt to consider the individual as the foundation of the state, and even
to suppose that it is formed by a number of separate individuals joining
together to form a body politic. We consider only individuals and the
state to be normal or necessary parts of any society. Of course, we might
admit various private and voluntary organizations, from clubs to political
parties to labor unions and trade associations. But all of these are private,
essentially nothing more than groups of individuals having no more status
in the constitution of society than a chance gathering of friends.

The lack of any other types of organizations has been detrimental to
both the state and to individual persons, for it has meant that the state,
and usually the central government, has had to concern itself with many
matters of detail that it should not have to bother with. Pius XI proposes
a different approach to societal problems:

> It is a fundamental principle of social philosophy, fixed and unchange-
> able, that one should not withdraw from individuals and commit to

> the community what they can accomplish by their own enterprise
> and industry. So, too, it is an injustice and at the same time a grave
> evil and a disturbance of right order, to transfer to the larger and
> higher collectivity functions which can be performed and provided
> for by lesser and subordinate bodies. Inasmuch as every social activ-
> ity should, by its very nature, prove a help to members of the body
> social, it should never destroy or absorb them. (no. 79)

This is the principle of subsidiarity, and by it the pontiff proposes that
necessary tasks be performed at the lowest level at which they can properly
be done. Pope Pius is not speaking here primarily about for-profit firms
or purely voluntary associations, but rather about other types of bodies
that should be established or restored and that can take on some of the
work we tend to associate with government only. For when he speaks of
the "social life which once flourished," he is referring to the guilds of the
Middle Ages and thereafter, which provided a means of organizing and
regulating commercial and industrial life, and which were also powerful
and wealthy institutions that at times could oppose a tyrannical ruler. These
guilds and other similar institutions helped to fill the void that modern
society has created, where there are only "individuals and the State."

Pius is calling for something like an updated version of the guilds, for
he advocates that all those who practice the same profession or who work
in the same industry join into occupational groups, to seek both their own
prosperity and the common good of the entire nation.

> For as nature induces those who dwell in close proximity to unite into
> municipalities, so those who practice the same trade or profession,
> economic or otherwise, constitute as it were fellowships or bodies.
> These groupings, autonomous in character, are considered by many
> to be, if not essential to civil society, at least a natural accompaniment
> thereof. (no. 83)

Such "fellowships or bodies" are not the same as our trade unions or
trade associations. For they must bind "men together not according to
the position they occupy in the labor market, but according to the diverse
functions which they exercise in society" (no. 83). In other words, *everyone* who works in the same industry, managers and workers, will be part
of that industry's occupational group. Unlike labor unions or employer

associations, necessary as both these groups may often be, occupational groups are to express the natural functional groupings of society, not class conflict between owner and worker. For everyone who makes his living in a particular industry must draw his livelihood from that industry's prosperity. From the company president to the mailroom messenger, each is rightly concerned, in different degrees, with the prosperity of the industry, and hence is interested in the industry's markets, sources of supplies, potential customers, and technology—in everything that contributes to the industry's health and profits. In addition, the members of the industry ought to be interested in whether and how the industry as a whole serves the common good.

> From this it is easy to conclude that in these associations the common interest of the whole "group" must predominate: and among these interests the most important is the directing of the activities of the group to the common good. (no. 85)

Although an association of pornographers or abortionists could well be concerned with the success of their industry, they could not direct their activities toward the common good, since by nature pornography and abortion harm the common good. Thus it behooves each industry or profession to make sure that the products or services that it produces or provides are truly helpful to society as a whole, not simply a means of enriching the individual producers and workers.

What sorts of activities will these occupational groups engage in? Some of them were suggested by Leo XIII himself in *Rerum Novarum*, when he stated that questions of wages and "the hours of labor in different trades, the sanitary precautions to be observed in factories and workshops," and like matters should be handled by joint employer/employee boards (no. 45). Pius does not himself propose any other duties for these groups here, but in addition to those recommended by Leo XIII, many commentators have suggested that they deal with questions such as prices of their products and the market share of participating firms. In the end, they are to reorient economic life so that different firms, as well as their managers and workers, regard themselves as brothers working together to serve the public, not as competitors or rivals trying to grab as large a share of the pot as possible.

Before finishing this middle section of *Quadragesimo Anno*, Pius XI brings up what he calls a "closely related aim." This is the orienting of economic activity according to its true principles. Here Pius is very clear and firm. He absolutely condemns the notion that free competition can be the ruling principle in the economy:

> Just as the unity of human society cannot be built upon "class" conflict, so the proper ordering of economic affairs cannot be left to the free play of rugged competition. From this source, as from a polluted spring, have proceeded all the errors of the "individualistic" school. This school, forgetful or ignorant of the social and moral aspects of economic activities, regarded these as completely free and immune from any intervention by public authority, for they would have in the market place and in unregulated competition a principle of self-direction more suitable for guiding them than any created intellect that might intervene. Free competition, however, though justified and quite useful within certain limits, cannot be an adequate controlling principle in economic affairs. This has been abundantly proved by the consequences that have followed from the free rein given to these dangerous individualistic ideas. It is therefore very necessary that economic affairs be once more subjected to and governed by a true and effective guiding principle. (no. 88)

In the first place, this passage makes it clear that no Catholic may accept free competition as arbiter of the market and economic activity. Instead, such activity must be ruled by the principles that Pius speaks of here. What principles are they? Social justice and social charity. Earlier the pontiff had introduced the concept of social justice and had stated that "the good of the whole community must be safeguarded. By these principles of social justice one class is forbidden to exclude the other from a share in the profits" (no. 57). Social justice, then, demands that society—and in particular the economy—be organized so that it itself promotes the good of the whole and of each of the parts. Pius XI insists that the law must enforce such a just organization of social life.

> To that end all the institutions of public and social life must be imbued with the spirit of justice, and this justice must above all be truly operative. It must build up a juridical and social order able to pervade all economic activity. (no. 88)

On the one hand, the laws of the nation must enforce this social justice, but on the other hand, "social life," the actual institutions under which people live, must also promote and embody justice. Moreover, "social charity should be, as it were, the soul of this order" (ibid.). Any nation attempting to create a just social order must actually enforce social justice with the power of the state. But beyond that, a charity akin to that charity animating the Mystical Body of Christ must permeate this order, so that we strive to give each one his due, not primarily out of fear of punishment, but because we regard our fellow contributors to the economic well-being of our nation as brothers, not as foes or rivals.

Then follows a short discussion of the economy of Fascist Italy (nos. 91–96). Though obviously of little practical relevance today, it is interesting to note Pius's comments, which, while not always favorable, are basically couched in a friendly tone. Mussolini had begun to establish something he called the corporate state, and the corporations in question here, "composed of representatives of the unions of workingmen and employers of the same trade or profession" (no. 93), bear some resemblance to the occupational groups Pius advocated.[2] Pius, however, criticizes Mussolini's corporations for being overly bureaucratic and political, since they were organs of the Italian state and subservient to Fascist policy. It should be noted that the pontiff discussed the economic system that was in place and suggested improvements. He was not thereby indicating his total approval. Similarly, when John Paul II, in *Centesimus Annus*, comments in a friendly way on the global capitalist order that we have today, we must not suppose that his suggestions for improving that order indicate that he regards capitalism as the best economic arrangement possible. I will discuss this at length in chapter five and appendix II.

In the third and last part of *Quadragesimo Anno*, Pius XI discusses three topics: the present state of the economy, socialism, and the reform of morals. The first and one of the most interesting points Pius XI makes in this section is his definition or characterization of capitalism: "that economic system in which [are] provided by different people the capital and labor jointly needed for production" (no. 100). That is, the defining note of capitalism is not private ownership or private economic initiative, but the separation of ownership and labor, the system in which, generally speaking, some people provide the capital and hire others to work for them. He does

---

2 Corporation, here, is from the Latin *corporatio*, meaning society or corporate body, and does not refer to a business corporation, as the term is used in the English-speaking world.

not condemn this separation of ownership and labor, as such, but he is severely critical of the actual state and operation of the capitalist economy.

> In the first place, then, it is patent that in our days not alone is wealth accumulated, but immense power and despotic economic domination is concentrated in the hands of a few, and that those few are frequently not the owners, but only the trustees and directors of invested funds, who administer them at their good pleasure. (no. 105)
>
> This power becomes particularly irresistible when exercised by those who, because they hold and control money, are able also to govern credit and determine its allotment, for that reason supplying, so to speak, the life-blood to the entire economic body, and grasping, as it were, in their hands the very soul of the economy, so that no one dare breathe against their will. (no. 106)
>
> This accumulation of power, a characteristic note of the modern economic order, is a natural result of unrestrained free competition which permits the survival of those only who are the strongest. This often means those who fight most relentlessly, who pay least heed to the dictates of conscience. (no. 107)

He sums up: "the whole economic life has become hard, cruel and relentless in a ghastly measure" (no. 109).

Although our economy is not in the same state as it was during the Great Depression when Pius XI wrote, we should not suppose that it has been fundamentally reformed so as to avoid the pontiff's condemnations. Many still champion free competition as the means of regulating the economy, and one need only look at the newspapers to see that the most successful are often "those who fight most relentlessly, who pay least heed to the dictates of conscience." Moreover, in recent decades the distribution of wealth and income has become increasingly skewed in favor of the very rich, while the economic situation for the rest of the population has become increasingly insecure.

After this discussion of the capitalist economy, the pope examines its chief rival, socialism. He notes that since the time of Leo XIII, socialism had divided into two sections, communism and more moderate socialism. He takes up the question (much discussed in the 1930s) as to how compatible socialism was or could be—especially in its moderate form—with the Catholic faith. His judgment on this question is well known: "No one can be at the same time a sincere Catholic and a true socialist" (no. 120). But his reasons for that judgment are less well known. Many people imagine that the reason for the impossibility of a Catholic being a true socialist has to do with the economic doctrines of socialism. But this is not primarily the case. As I just noted, Pius indicates that in his day socialism had divided into two parts, and he points out that the economic proposals of some of the moderate socialists "often strikingly approach the just demands of Christian social reformers" (no. 113). As an example, he notes and approves the contention of these moderate socialists that "certain forms of property must be reserved to the State, since they carry with them an opportunity of domination too great to be left to private individuals without injury to the community at large" (no. 114). He goes on to say: "Just demands and desires of this kind contain nothing opposed to Christian truth…" (no. 115). If this is so, what is the problem with socialism? Why cannot "a sincere Catholic" be "a true socialist"? It is because socialism "conceives human society in a way utterly alien to Christian truth" (no. 117). Socialism, he explains, is

> entirely ignorant of or unconcerned about [the] sublime end both of individuals and of society, affirms that living in community was instituted merely for the sake of advantages which it brings to mankind. (no. 118)

In the next section he makes it clear that it is *material* advantages that are in question here. For if it were the case "that living in community was instituted merely for the sake of [material] advantages," then the end of society would be simply more and more material goods. This, however, is contrary both to right reason (which recognizes that material goods are meant to serve human welfare and thus are subordinate to it) and to papal teaching (expressed, for example, by Leo XIII in *Rerum Novarum*) that "since it is the end of society to make men better, the chief good that society can be possessed of is virtue" (no. 34). But whatever the beliefs or opinions of any individual calling himself a socialist, Pius is clear that

> whether socialism be considered as a doctrine, or as a historical fact, or as a "movement," if it really remains socialism, it cannot be brought into harmony with the dogmas of the Catholic Church, even after it has yielded to truth and justice in the points We have mentioned;

the reason being that it conceives human society in a way utterly
alien to Christian truth. (no. 117)

Actual existing socialism has always been hostile to the Christian conception of society and culture, and there is no point in trying to rehabilitate or
claim a term with such negative historical associations, even though many
socialists had begun to embrace economic doctrines that "often strikingly
approach the just demands of Christian social reformers" (no. 113).

One point that is little noticed, however, is that this teaching of Pope
Leo and Pope Pius conflicts not only with socialism, but also with much
of the rhetoric that is used to justify capitalism. How often, for example,
is capitalism praised and justified because it has created great material
wealth? As we will see in chapter five, John Paul II notes this connection
between capitalism and materialism in his encyclical *Centesimus Annus*.

Next, Pope Pius turns to the question of moral reform, without which
the "social edifice will be built, not upon a rock, but upon shifting sand"
(no. 127). Here the pontiff denounces "that unquenchable thirst for riches
and temporal possessions," which has always afflicted man, but points out
that "the economic world today lays more snares than ever for human
frailty." Among others he lists "easy returns, which an open market offers
to any one," and the "divided responsibility and limited liability" of corporations that "have given occasion to abominable abuses" (no. 132). "A stern
insistence on the moral law, enforced with vigor by civil authority, could
have dispelled or perhaps averted these enormous evils" (no. 133). One
can see that the pontiff does not separate completely the moral reform
of individuals from state action on behalf of justice. Rather, he continues
and points out that the reconstruction of the social order called for by
this encyclical, including the institution of occupational groups, cannot
succeed without redirecting man's desires.

> All those versed in social matters demand a rationalization of eco-
> nomic life which will restore a sound and true order. But this order,
> which We Ourselves desire and make every effort to promote, will
> necessarily be quite faulty and imperfect, unless all man's activities
> harmoniously unite to imitate and, as far as humanly possible, attain
> the marvelous unity of the divine plan. This is the perfect order
> which the Church preaches, with intense earnestness, and which
> right reason demands: which places God as the first and supreme

end of all created activity, and regards all created goods as mere instruments under God, to be used only in so far as they help toward the attainment of our supreme end. (no. 136)

A little later he again reminds us that charity, while no substitute for justice, is its necessary accompaniment. "Charity cannot take the place of justice unfairly withheld, but, even though a state of things be pictured in which every man receives at last all that is his due, a wide field will nevertheless remain open for charity" (no. 137).

Pius XI is calling for nothing less than a remaking of society, the "reconstruction of the social order." He knows it will be a difficult undertaking.

> And in truth, the world has nowadays sore need of valiant soldiers of Christ, who strain every thew and sinew to preserve the human family from the dire havoc which would befall it were the teachings of the Gospel to be flouted, and a social order permitted to prevail, which spurns no less the laws of nature than those of God. (no. 144)

This encyclical presents an entire doctrine for social reconstruction, and a picture of a world remade on Christian principles. Lest we think it is only a pretty picture, but one unattainable in this world, we should remember that Pius himself censured those who thought *Rerum Novarum* was "a utopian ideal, desirable rather than attainable in practice" (no. 14). Though now the difficulties of establishing a just society are many times greater than in 1931, still we must make whatever strides toward it that we can. We can never simply nod our heads and pass on to other things, thinking that this is not an important area of Christian morality or apostolic endeavor. Still worse is the response of any who would argue and quibble at the pontiff's words, while still supposing themselves good Catholics.

> Let, then, all men of good will stand united. Let all those who, under the pastors of the Church, wish to fight this good and peaceful fight of Christ, as far as talents, powers and station allow, strive to play their part in the Christian renewal of human society.... (no. 147)

Even if we achieve little in this "good and peaceful fight," we will be making our offering of the world to the Heart of Jesus Christ more perfect, and more pleasing to the Redeemer of men and nations.

Although *Quadragesimo Anno* was Pius XI's most systematic treatment of social doctrine, his 1937 encyclical, *Divini Redemptoris*, was also a notable achievement in the social field. This encyclical is somewhat neglected today, mostly because its chief topic is atheistic communism, and after the collapse of nearly all Communist regimes its importance may not be obvious. But because Pius XI always looked at contemporary matters in light of fundamental principles, there is much in *Divini Redemptoris* that is relevant today, since Pius points out again the many failings of capitalist commercial civilization, most of which are still present.

Pope Pius XI, as demonstrated in *Quadragesimo Anno*, was well aware of the deficiencies of capitalism, and as a result he saw that communism was able to make headway in his day "by urging the removal of the very real abuses chargeable to the liberalistic economic order, and by demanding a more equitable distribution of this world's goods (objects entirely and undoubtedly legitimate)..." (no. 15).[3] But in order to achieve such a "removal of the very real abuses chargeable to the liberalistic economic order, and...a more equitable distribution of this world's goods," according to the teaching of the Church, Pius XI is more explicit even than he was in *Quadragesimo Anno* about how the economy should be organized. Referring to that encyclical, Pius writes here of the need for

> the infusion of social justice and the sentiment of Christian love into the socio-economic order. We have indicated how a sound prosperity is to be restored according to the true principles of a sane corporative system which respects the proper hierarchic structure of society; and how all the occupational groups should be fused into a harmonious whole inspired by the principle of the common good. (no. 32)

---

3 It is vital to recognize that the term *liberal* and its derivatives, as they are employed here by Pius XI and generally in papal writings, are used in the European sense and bear a different meaning from their American usage. Liberalism in this sense, as Paul VI pointed out in *Octogesima Adveniens*, "believes it exalts individual freedom by withdrawing it from every limitation, by stimulating it through exclusive seeking of interest and power, and by considering social solidarities as more or less automatic consequences of individual initiatives, not as an aim and a major criterion of the value of the social organization" (no. 26). It is more or less equivalent in economic matters to the classical liberalism of the Manchester school of economics condemned by Leo XIII or the "rigid capitalism" denounced by John Paul II. Liberalism in this sense champions freedom, particularly in economic affairs. Today it is often called *neo-liberalism*. Most of those who in the United States are called conservatives are really liberals in this respect.

And addressing a point that even today is controversial, Pope Pius states that

> in the sphere of social-economics, although the Church has never
> proposed a definite technical system, since this is not her field,
> she has nevertheless clearly outlined the guiding principles which,
> while susceptible of varied concrete applications according to the
> diversified conditions of times and places and peoples, indicate the
> safe way of securing the happy progress of society. (no. 34)

Some commentators will interpret this statement, and the parallel passage in
Quadragesimo Anno (nos. 41–43), to mean that the Church's social doctrine
constitutes merely a set of vague goals. But such an interpretation cannot be
maintained. Pius XI is explicit in this encyclical about a "sane corporative
system." Later he speaks of the medieval guilds and notes that they "are
today claiming the admiration of our contemporaries in many countries
who are endeavoring to revive them in some modern form" (no. 37). It
is impossible to understand Pius as simply recommending generalities.
Rather he mandates certain specific types of institutions, even if he rightly
does not claim the ability to prescribe their nature and functions in detail.

In *Quadragesimo Anno*, Pope Pius had taught that "charity cannot
take the place of justice unfairly withheld" (no. 137), and here he states
even more sternly that "a 'charity' which deprives the workingman of the
salary to which he has a strict title in justice is not charity at all, but only
its empty name and hollow semblance" (no. 49). One should especially
note the assertion, "the salary to which he has a strict title in justice." This
means that the worker has a right in *commutative* justice, the justice of
exact exchange, not merely in distributive or social justice, which concern
society as a whole. Although there are times when an employer's duty in
strict justice is suspended,[4] it is not suspended when the employer has the
ability to pay such wages. Moreover, whenever the duty in commutative
justice to pay a just wage is suspended, it is replaced by another duty,
namely the duty in *social* justice to work to reform the economy so that
a just wage can in fact be paid.

> All too frequently…under the salary system,…individual employers
> are helpless to ensure justice unless, with a view to its practice, they

---

4 See *Quadragesimo Anno*, nos. 71–73.

This task of the Church is indeed arduous, but they are simply unwit-
ting deserters or dupes who, in deference to a misguided supernat-
uralism, would confine the Church to the "strictly religious" field,
as they say, whereas by so doing they are but playing into the hands
of their enemies.
    — Address to members of Rinascita Cristiana, January 22, 1947

On the question of the place of competition in economic affairs, Pius XII,
echoing *Quadragesimo Anno*, had this to say:

> The demands of competition, which is a normal consequence of
> human liberty and ingenuity, cannot be the final norm for economics.
>   — Address to International Foundry Congress,
>   September 28, 1954

All this is no more than a taste of the many rich and varied comments
that Pius XII made on social questions during his pontificate. They show,
as one would expect, that he taught the same doctrine as his predecessors,
building on the foundations of social doctrine laid by Leo XIII and Pius XI.

After the death of Pius XII, St. John XXIII was elevated to the papacy
in October of 1958. His one encyclical devoted entirely to the economic
order was *Mater et Magistra*, issued May 15, 1961. I will mention only
the salient points of this document, which in many ways forms a bridge
between the teaching of Pius XI and Pius XII, and that of Paul VI and
John Paul II.

Pope John begins his encyclical by recalling that "the teaching of
Christ joins, as it were, earth with heaven, in that it embraces the whole
man,...body and soul" (no. 2). Just as Our Lord "was moved to exclaim
sorrowfully, 'I have compassion on the crowd'" (no. 4) before he fed
them in the wilderness, his Church has continued to care for both the
bodies and souls of men. He added that the encyclical of Leo XIII, *Rerum
Novarum*, is "notable evidence" (no. 7) of the Church's charitable concern
for mankind.

The pontiff briefly recites the circumstances of *Rerum Novarum*'s
origins and effects, and then summarizes its contents, as well as those
of *Quadragesimo Anno* and several social messages of Pius XII. After
pointing out that circumstances have changed greatly since these earlier
social documents, he writes:

> We feel it our duty to keep alive the torch lighted by our great pre-
> decessors and to exhort all to draw from their writings light and
> inspiration, if they wish to resolve the social question in ways more
> in accord with the needs of the present time. (no. 50)

One of the things that prompted St. John XXIII to issue this encyclical
was the increasing complexity of social and economic life, "a daily more
complex interdependence of citizens, introducing into their lives and
activities many and varied forms of association" (no. 59). These in turn
cause a "growing intervention of public authorities" (no. 60). But because
of this increased activity on the part of private organizations and firms
and of the state:

> it becomes difficult for one to make decisions independently of
> outside influences, to do anything on his own initiative, to carry
> out in a fitting way his rights and duties, and to fully develop and
> perfect his personality. Will men perhaps then become automatons,
> and cease to be personally responsible, as these social relationships
> multiply more and more? It is a question which must be answered
> negatively. (no. 62)

Pope John reminds us that this increasing social complexity does not
result "from a blind drive of natural forces" (no. 63), but that man is free.
With this he touches on a theme that has been developed much more by
John Paul II, namely, the centrality of the human person in social and
economic processes. In *Mater et Magistra*, the pope uses this criterion
of the human person as his standard for evaluating all socio-economic
arrangements and structures.

> Consequently, if the organization and structure of economic life be
> such that the human dignity of workers is compromised, or their sense
> of responsibility is weakened, or their freedom of action is removed,
> then we judge such an economic order to be unjust, even though it
> produces a vast amount of goods, whose distribution conforms to
> the norms of justice and equity. (no. 83)

In accord with this teaching, and in order to preserve and create types
of businesses in which the dignity of man could more easily be upheld,

John XXIII several times recommends the fostering of small and craft enterprises, cooperatives, and family farms. He devotes much space to discussing appropriate means of aiding them in a modern economy, including professional associations and "special provision for them" by the state "in regard to instruction, taxes, credit facilities, social security and insurance" (no. 88).

Although the social encyclicals of Leo XIII and Pius XI had more than once touched on the international aspects of the social question, both of those pontiffs had largely confined their focus to national economies. But as trade between nations increased, so did other aspects of international economic relations, including foreign aid and the beginnings of international economic organizations, such as the International Labor Organization, the World Bank, and many others. Thus, the Church naturally had to turn her attention to these activities and organizations, for they raise many questions of justice and human dignity. In *Mater et Magistra*, Pope John begins the first major papal discussion of these international questions, a discussion that will be developed by Paul VI, John Paul II, and Benedict XVI.

The pope discusses the economic dealings between rich and poor countries, foreign aid, the relation of population to economic development, and the root of international distrust and conflict. He points out that some, "more especially leaders of States" (no. 205), disagree about truth and right; though they use words such as "justice," different leaders mean different things by them. But, the pontiff reminds us, "the guiding principles of morality and virtue can be based only on God; apart from Him, they necessarily collapse" (no. 207). This leads him into a discussion of materialism and other false philosophies. Some, for example, think that the progress of science and technology means that man can forget God, and therefore "no folly seems more characteristic of our time than the desire to establish a firm and meaningful temporal order, but without God, its necessary foundation" (no. 217). To counter this, the social teaching of the Church is "not only to be explained but also applied" (no. 226). He concludes his encyclical by exhorting all involved in the lay apostolate to dedicate themselves to this task.

> We desire that the divine Redeemer of mankind, "who has become for us God-given wisdom, and justice, and sanctification, and redemption," may reign and triumph gloriously in all things and over all

things, for centuries on end. We desire that, in a properly organized
order of social affairs, all nations will at last enjoy prosperity, and
happiness, and peace. (no. 263)

With this John XXIII concludes *Mater et Magistra*. John's reign was followed
by that of Blessed Paul VI, whose social documents we will take up now.

Paul VI (1963–1978) succeeded to the papacy in the midst of the most
noteworthy ecclesiastical event of the twentieth century, the Second Vatican
Council. Vatican II was opened by John XXIII on October 11, 1962, but he
died in June of 1963 after only the first session. The Council completed its
work under Pope Paul. The Council did not issue a document explicitly and
entirely on the subject of social doctrine, but there are sections of *Gaudium
et Spes* (*Pastoral Constitution on the Church in the Modern World*), issued
on December 7, 1965, that deal with social teaching.

Briefly, in *Gaudium et Spes*, the Council Fathers propose to "reiterate
[the principles of the Church's social teaching] in accordance with the situation of the world today" and to "outline certain guidelines, particularly
with reference to the requirements of economic development" (no. 63).[2]
They first turned their attention to man himself, for whom the economy
exists. The Fathers were thus concerned with anything that directed
economic activity away from man (no. 64). As a result, *Gaudium et Spes*
warns against an economy that is dominated and managed by only a few
persons, thereby creating the "immense economic inequalities which exist
in the world and increase from day to day" (no. 66). The Council Fathers
reaffirm the freedom and right of individuals to form and join associations
to preserve and to further their economic well-being.

Furthermore, since "God destined the earth and all it contains for all
men and all peoples" (no. 69), economic processes must serve and not
frustrate that purpose. Thus "investment…should be directed to providing
employment and ensuring sufficient income for the people of today and of
the future" (no. 70), and the "social dimension" of private property must
not be forgotten. In areas with large numbers of poor where there exist
"large and sometimes very extensive rural estates which are only slightly
cultivated or not cultivated at all," it can be lawful for the "competent
authority" to expropriate these estates in order to provide land for the
poor, with compensation for their prior owners (no. 71).

2 Quotations from *Gaudium et Spes* are from Austin Flannery, ed., *Vatican Council II, Vol.
1: The Conciliar and Post Conciliar Documents* (Collegeville, MN: Liturgical Press, 1975).

Turning to the social documents of Paul VI, let us first explore his encyclical *Populorum Progressio*. Paul VI issued this encyclical on Easter Sunday, March 26, 1967. While John XXIII in *Mater et Magistra* had given considerable attention to the international aspects of the social question, Pope Paul devotes his entire letter to it. At the very beginning of *Populorum Progressio* the pontiff proclaims: "Today the principal fact that we must all recognize is that the social question has become world-wide" (no. 3). Thus justice and charity *among* nations rather than within individual nations is his subject.

Many of the social encyclicals were occasioned by crises in the world. Leo XIII wrote in *Rerum Novarum*, for example, that "some remedy must be found, and quickly found, for the misery and wretchedness which press so heavily at this moment on the large majority of the very poor" (no. 3). But *Populorum Progressio*, perhaps more than any other encyclical, is a personal appeal by the sovereign pontiff in the face of the world's need, a real *cri de coeur*, a cry of the heart. As he says at the end of the encyclical (no. 87): "Yes, We ask you, all of you, to heed Our cry of anguish, in the name of the Lord." The pope notes how his own journeys to poor regions "brought Us into direct contact with the acute problems" (no. 4) of those nations.

> Today no one can be ignorant any longer of the fact that in whole continents countless men and women are ravished by hunger, countless numbers of children are undernourished, so that many of them die in infancy, while the physical growth and mental development of many others are retarded and as a result whole regions are condemned to the most depressing despondency. (no. 45)

And so this encyclical is devoted to the *progressio* — usually translated as "development" — of the peoples of the world. But development means more than increased riches. "Development cannot be limited to mere economic growth. In order to be authentic, it must be complete: integral, that is, it has to promote the good of every man and of the whole man" (no. 14). He even goes so far as to say:

> Increased possession is not the ultimate goal of nations nor of individuals. All growth is ambivalent. It is essential if man is to develop as a man, but in a way it imprisons man if he considers it the supreme good, and it restricts his vision. (no. 19)

Blessed Paul VI is concerned, then, with man on every level, and is eager to impart guidance and exhortation for genuine progress. He points out, in fact, that when poorer countries receive aid from rich countries, they are apt to imitate the materialism of their benefactors and to lose their own spiritual and cultural traditions in the name of material progress. "Less well-off peoples can never be sufficiently on their guard against this temptation which comes to them from wealthy nations" (no. 41).

It is still true, however, that much needs to be done on a material level. Pope Paul insists again on the justice and charity that Leo XIII and Pius XI had earlier demanded. Just as Leo XIII, for instance, had said that "the earth, though divided among private owners, ceases not thereby to minister to the needs of all,"[3] Paul VI similarly teaches: "If the world is made to furnish each individual with the means of livelihood..., each man has therefore the right to find in the world what is necessary for himself" (no. 22). The world was created to sustain all of mankind, and our economic arrangements, our "rights... of property and of free commerce, are to be subordinated to this principle" (no. 22). Of course this does not mean that all goods are simply to be held in common. Rather it means that if we find that the structures we have created to carry on our economic life are actually making it more difficult for all people to gain a reasonable living for themselves and their families, then it is these structures that must be changed, for "the economy is at the service of man" (no. 26).

And just as Pius XI noted in *Quadragesimo Anno* the social duties of private property (nos. 45–49) and wrote that "the proper ordering of economic affairs cannot be left to the free play of rugged competition" (no. 88), Paul VI similarly teaches that

> it is unfortunate that...a system has been constructed which considers profit as the key motive for economic progress, competition as the supreme law of economics, and private ownership of the means of production as an absolute right that has no limits and carries no corresponding social obligations. (no. 26)

Because of changed conditions in the world economy, Paul VI brings out what was only implicit in earlier papal teaching: namely, that the same

---

3 *Rerum Novarum*, no. 8.

requirements of justice that obtain between individuals and groups within a national economy must also obtain between different countries.

> What was true of the just wage for the individual is also true of international contracts: an economy of exchange can no longer be based solely on the law of free competition.... Freedom of trade is fair only if it is subject to the demands of social justice. (no. 59)

Leo XIII had taught that insofar as a man's labor is necessary to provide for himself and his family, "each one has a right to procure what is required in order to live; and the poor can procure it in no other way than by work and wages."[4] Thus a wage agreement that does not provide what the worker and his family need is unjust even if it has been agreed upon in apparent freedom. In a similar way, Pope Paul points out that international trade cannot be permitted to impoverish poor countries, which often rely on the export of raw materials that are "subject to wide and sudden fluctuations in price" (no. 57). "As a result, nations whose industrialisation is limited are faced with serious difficulties when they have to rely on their exports to balance their economy and to carry out their plans for development" (ibid.). If the prices for industrial goods remain stable or increase, but the prices of raw materials decrease, a situation arises in which "poor nations remain ever poor while the rich ones become still richer" (ibid.). In a passage still relevant today, he discusses international debt, remarking that loans must be "conditioned by the real needs of the receiving countries" and that if done properly and justly, poor countries

> will...no longer risk being overwhelmed by debts whose repayment swallows up the greater part of their gains. Rates of interest and time for repayment of the loan could be so arranged as not to be too great a burden on either party, taking into account free gifts, interest-free or low-interest loans, and the time needed for liquidating the debts. (no. 54)

In the face of all these needs, Pope Paul calls on the world to develop the charity and solidarity that are needed as a remedy.

---

4 *Rerum Novarum*, no. 44.

> The world is sick. Its illness consists less in the unproductive monop-
> olisation of resources by a small number of men than in the lack of
> brotherhood among individuals and peoples. (no. 66)

Even the peace of the world is threatened by the disparity between
the rich and the poor nations. "Excessive economic, social and cultural
inequalities among peoples arouse tensions and conflicts, and are a danger
to peace" (no. 76). But in the unity of the human race we are all brothers,
called to contribute to the needs and advancement of all.

> We ask Our Catholic sons who belong to the more favored nations
> to bring their talents and give their active participation to organ-
> isations...which are working to overcome the difficulties of the
> developing nations. (no. 81)
>   All of you who have heard the appeal of suffering peoples, all of
> you who are working to answer their cries, you are the apostles of a
> development which is good and genuine, which is not wealth that
> is self-centered and sought for its own sake, but rather an economy
> which is put at the service of man, the bread which is daily distributed
> to all, as a source of brotherhood and a sign of Providence. (no. 86)

On this note the pope proceeds to his conclusion. Just as Leo XIII pleaded
for justice and charity for the workingman, so Paul VI pleads for justice
and charity for the poor of this earth.

Although Paul VI did not issue any more social encyclicals, I will
briefly discuss one more social document of his reign — the apostolic
letter *Octogesima Adveniens*, issued on May 14, 1971, in commemoration
of the eightieth anniversary of *Rerum Novarum*.

In this letter Pope Paul touches on a great number of questions, "questions which because of their urgency, extent and complexity must in the
years to come take first place among the preoccupations of Christians..."
(no. 7). Thus in this letter the pope takes note of problems that in 1971 were
current or just emerging as major issues. These include the beginning of
huge mega-cities in Third World countries, the youth revolt of the 1960s,
changes in the role of women, and the increased concern for the natural
environment. After this survey, the pontiff speaks of the various ideologies,
such as socialism, communism, and the "renewal of the liberal ideology."
He notes "that at the very root of philosophical liberalism is an erroneous

affirmation of the autonomy of the individual in his activity, his motivation and the exercise of his liberty" (no. 35).

Issuing "a fresh and insistent call" to "all Christians," the pope calls on Catholics to draw upon the Church's social teachings to avoid the errors that are present in these ideologies. Quoting his own encyclical *Populorum Progressio*, he states: "Laymen should take up as their own proper task the renewal of the temporal order" (no. 48). This is necessary if the love of God is to become known by all.

> Today more than ever the Word of God will be unable to be proclaimed and heard unless it is accompanied by the witness of the power of the Holy Spirit, working within the action of Christians in the service of their brothers.... (no. 51)

Many of Blessed Paul's concerns — such as the international debt of poor countries, the "renewal of the liberal ideology," and the materialism of both rich and poor nations — are concerns that still affect us today and were shared by John Paul II, whose teaching we will consider in the next chapter.

FOUR

John Paul II,
Laborem Exercens and
Sollicitudo Rei Socialis

I WILL BEGIN THE DISCUSSION OF THE SOCIAL ENCYC-licals of St. John Paul II with his first two, *Laborem Exercens* and *Sollicitudo Rei Socialis*. John Paul II began his reign in October of 1978 after the brief pontificate of John Paul I (August to September 1978). As is well known, John Paul II was the first non-Italian pope since 1523 and the first Pole ever chosen as Vicar of Christ. John Paul II's encyclicals and other writings have often been longer and more meditative than those of previous pontiffs. In a sense, he has created a body of work that is a con-sciously interrelated statement of the faith. He himself often pointed out the connection of one dogma with another: for example, the relationship between the Church's doctrine of the nature of man and her doctrine of man's rights and duties in society.[1]

Pope John Paul intended to issue *Laborem Exercens* on May 15, 1981, the ninetieth anniversary of *Rerum Novarum*. But because of the attempt on his life on May 13, he was not able to revise it until after he left the hos-pital, and thus it was not issued until September 14 of that year. *Laborem Exercens* is a sustained reflection on the meaning of human work, which John Paul considers to be *"a key,* probably *the essential key,* to the whole social question..." (no. 3).[2] In this document he is more interested in looking at social teaching in the light of the concept of work, rather than in formulating new norms for a changed social situation. As we examine the main points of his reflections, we will more clearly see his insights into the meaning of the Church's social doctrine.

---

1 For example, see the encyclical *Redemptor Hominis*, no. 14.
2 The emphasis in the quoted texts in this and the following chapters are those of the original texts.

John Paul is interested in work because he is interested in man. For man has been given the task of work from the beginning.

> The Church finds *in the very first pages of the book of Genesis* the source of her conviction that work is a fundamental dimension of human existence on earth. An analysis of these texts makes us aware that they express…the fundamental truths about man, in the context of the mystery of creation itself. These truths are decisive for man from the very beginning, and at the same time they trace out the main lines of his earthly existence, both in the state of original justice and also after the breaking, caused by sin, of the Creator's original covenant with creation in man. When man, who had been created "in the image of God…male and female," hears the words: "*Be fruitful and multiply, and fill the earth and subdue it,*" even though these words do not refer directly and explicitly to work, beyond any doubt they indirectly indicate it as an activity for man to carry out in the world. Indeed, they show its very deepest essence. Man is the image of God partly through the mandate received from his Creator to subdue, to dominate, the earth. In carrying out this mandate, man, every human being, reflects the very action of the Creator of the universe. (no. 4)

This quotation captures the essence of the doctrine of St. John Paul about the origins of human work and man's duty to work. Since work is something that has resulted from God's creation of man, it is connected with what man himself is, with how he was originally constituted by his Creator. In other words, we cannot understand work unless we first understand man. Since man was created by God, we can gain insight into man's nature and purpose by seeing the original plan for man as revealed in the book of Genesis. It is there that Pope John Paul sees our call to work.

In his discussion of work, John Paul makes a distinction that will be important throughout his entire argument: the difference between objective and subjective work. Work in the objective sense is simply the external aspects of work, the actual job one does, with its necessary tools or machines. Obviously work in this sense has changed drastically over the centuries, and differs considerably from one kind of work to another. But work in the subjective sense is something different; it is *man himself,* man as a worker and the subject of work.

> As a person he works, he performs various actions belonging to the
> work process; independently of their objective content, these actions
> must all serve to realize his humanity, to fulfill the calling to be a
> person that is his by reason of his very humanity. (no. 6)

Having established this notion of man as the subject of work, John
Paul uses it to examine various aspects of work and of the social question. For example, the pontiff points out that according to certain nineteenth-century theories,

> work was understood and treated as a sort of 'merchandise' that the
> worker... sells to the employer, who at the same time is the possessor
> of the capital, that is to say, of all the working tools and means that
> make production possible. (no. 7)

Any such approach, by which free persons are in a sense equated with
the material factors of production, is rooted in materialism[3] and is what
John Paul calls *economism*, which is the error "of considering human
labor solely according to its economic purpose" (no. 13). This is to look
only at the objective aspect of work — the kind of work to be done or the
economic value of the job — rather than at the subject of the work, man the
worker. The social question arose in the last century as a "reaction *against
the degradation of man as the subject of work*, and against the unheard-of
accompanying exploitation in the field of wages, working conditions and
social security for the worker" (no. 8).

Thus it is neglect of the subjective aspect of work, man himself, and
exclusive emphasis on its objective aspect, that has created the social question. One can see this in the question of wages, for example. If we look only
at the type of work being done or its place in the national economy, we
might conclude that certain work has only a limited economic value. But
if, on the other hand, we look at who is doing the work, free persons made
in the image of God, then we would have to grant them what is their due
because of their humanity — namely, the ability to live in human dignity
regardless of the low social status of their objective work.

From the above discussion we can see how St. John Paul II deduces

---

3 Materialism here can mean either philosophic materialism — the doctrine that only matter
exists — or practical materialism, which is to live as if only matter exists or as if only material
things are important.

an important principle of Catholic social doctrine, "a principle that has always been taught by the Church: *the principle of the priority of labor over capital*" (no. 12). This principle is true because it is based on the fact that man is an efficient cause in the process of production, "while capital, the whole collection of means of production, remains a mere *instrument* or instrumental cause." One can see from this, though, that John Paul is not using "capital" here as shorthand for "capitalists." Rather he means any *thing*, whether money, natural resources, tools, or machines, with which man works. These things are "placed at man's disposal. However, these resources *can serve man only through work*" (no. 12). Without man and without work, these lifeless things could not serve their purpose and be means to fulfill the commandment to subdue the earth.

If this is the case, how did the opposition arise between those who contribute labor to the production process, and those who contribute capital? This happened, John Paul says, because of the error of economism, the error "of considering human labor solely according to its economic purpose." In a

> time of the birth and rapid development of industrialization, in which what was mainly seen was the possibility of vastly increasing material wealth,...man, who should be served by [this wealth], was ignored. It was this practical error that *struck a blow* first and foremost against human labor, against *the working man*, and caused the ethically just social reaction. (no. 13)

In other words, because of the greed provoked by the opportunities for the unprecedented profits that the industrial revolution brought about, man (the subjective and most important factor in work) was relegated to a subordinate role based on the assumed economic value of his contribution to the productive process. The fact that absolutely no production of any kind could take place without man (who invents, designs, and operates machinery) was hardly noticed. Thus practical materialism caused a viewpoint that resulted in economism.

The Holy Father was certainly aware that in the conflict between capital and labor it is not impersonal forces, but "people, living, actual people" who are involved, and that "on the one side are those who do the work without being the owners of the means of production, and on the other side those who act as entrepreneurs and who own these means or represent the owners" (no. 14). This fact then raises the issue of property ownership—its rights, duties and morality.

John Paul, of course, restates the teaching of his predecessors regarding man's right to the ownership of private property, "even when it is a question of the means of production" (no. 14). And he notes that this teaching "*diverges* radically from the program of *collectivism* as proclaimed by Marxism…" (no. 14). But he also notes the following about Catholic teaching:

> At the same time it differs from the program of *capitalism* practiced by liberalism and by the political systems inspired by it. In the latter case, the difference consists in the way the right to ownership or property is understood. Christian tradition has never upheld this right as absolute and untouchable. On the contrary, it has always understood this right within the broader context of the right common to all to use the goods of the whole of creation: *the right to private property is subordinated to the right to common use*, to the fact that goods are meant for everyone. (no. 14)

Since all property is acquired originally by work, and the only purpose of property or capital is in the service of work—by furnishing the means with which men actually work and produce useful goods or services—it makes no sense to set labor and capital in opposition to each other. But it does make sense to ask questions about the arrangements of property ownership in order that property may in fact serve human work.

And so the pope reminds us that "one cannot exclude the *socialization*, in suitable conditions, of certain means of production" (no. 14). It is interesting, however, to see what he means by this statement. First, he is referring to state ownership, which of course can be legitimate, as Pius XI likewise taught.[4] He is not, however, referring to socialism—the socio-economic system condemned by Pius XI as incompatible with Catholicism.[5] Rather, he is bringing to light a more fundamental truth—often lost in the bitter political debates that characterize this subject—"that merely taking these means of production (capital) out of the hands of their private owners is not enough to ensure their satisfactory socialization" (no. 14). Here John Paul stands both capitalists and socialists on their heads. For although the problem of disregarding the subject of human work is real,

---

4 *Quadragesimo Anno*, no. 114.
5 Ibid., nos. 117 and 120.

it cannot be solved merely by subjecting the worker to state ownership
and a bureaucratic boss instead of private ownership and a corporate boss.
In both cases he can be exploited.

> We can speak of socializing only when the subject character of society
> is ensured, that is to say, when on the basis of his work each person is
> fully entitled to consider himself a part-owner of the great workbench
> at which he is working with every one else. (no. 14)

If state ownership is not the automatic solution of the problem, what
can be done? The pontiff makes many of the same proposals that were
made by Leo XIII, Pius XI and Pius XII, such as "associating labor with the
ownership of capital," and even makes a clear reference to the occupational
groups highlighted by Pius XI. He characterizes them as

> intermediate bodies with economic, social and cultural purposes;
> they would be bodies enjoying real autonomy with regard to the
> public powers, pursuing their specific aims in honest collaboration
> with each other and in subordination to the demands of the common
> good.... (no. 14)

Those who maintain that one or another type of legal arrangement of
property ownership, public or private, can solve all difficulties are wrong,
for neither the ideologues of collectivism nor of capitalism grasp that
specific steps must be taken so that the worker not "feel that he is just
a cog in a huge machine moved from above..." (no. 15). "The Church's
teaching has always expressed the strong and deep conviction that man's
work concerns not only the economy but also, and especially, personal
values" (no. 15). In other words, work is not just an economic action; it is
primarily something about the human person. It has economic consequences to be sure, but it arises from and affects man and society at many
levels deeper than the economic.

Next John Paul introduces the concept of the direct and indirect
employer. A direct employer is an employer according to the usual meaning. An indirect employer, on the other hand, "includes both persons and
institutions of various kinds, and also collective labor contracts...which
determine the whole socioeconomic *system*..." (no. 17). The concept can
perhaps be better understood by means of a quotation from Pius XI.

> If, however, the business does not make enough money to pay the
> workman a just wage, either because it is overwhelmed with unjust
> burdens, or because it is compelled to sell its products at an unjustly
> low price, those who thus injure it are guilty of grievous wrong; for
> it is they who deprive the workingmen of the just wage, and force
> them to accept lower terms.[6]

In other words, an employer or firm does not operate in a vacuum. The
ability to pay just wages, in fact the entire labor policy, depends on many
things over which an individual owner or corporation has little or no
control. These include government policies, the policies of other industries, unions, foreign governments and corporations, international institutions such as the World Bank or the International Monetary Fund, and
increasingly, international agreements concerning trade, the environment,
or other matters. All these are part of what John Paul calls the indirect
employer. And because of their importance and their influence on wages
and working conditions, these indirect employers have, to one degree
or another, a "true responsibility" (no. 17) for the resulting situation and
welfare of the workers. This includes the influence that the public and
private policies of rich countries can have on the economies of their poorer
trading partners and debtor countries.

   After making this distinction between the direct and indirect employer,
the pope begins a discussion of employment and unemployment. He
points out the duty of indirect employers "to meet the danger of unemployment and to ensure employment for all" by making "provision for
overall planning" (no. 18). "In the final analysis this overall concern
weighs on the shoulders of the State..." (ibid.). He adds, "but it cannot
mean one-sided centralization by the public authorities. Instead, what
is in question is a just and rational *coordination...*" (ibid.). This brings
to one's mind Pius XI's summary of the state's duties in the economic
realm: "directing, supervising, encouraging, restraining."[7] It can hardly
be overemphasized that the Church sees a role for the state in the economy different from that proposed by both conservatives and liberals, as
those terms are used in the United States. The state is not to step back
and merely maintain law and order. Instead, as the guardian of the common good of the nation, it must be concerned with the entire life of its

---

6 *Quadragesimo Anno*, no. 72. See also the encyclical *Divini Redemptoris*, nos. 53–54.

7 *Quadragesimo Anno*, no. 80.

citizens, but it by no means follows that the state should directly involve itself in every aspect of their lives.[8] Rather the public authorities are to direct, to supervise, to encourage, to restrain, and (as John Paul puts it) to coordinate the efforts of other groups—not only businesses, but also cooperatives, labor unions, occupational groups, and voluntary associations, which will themselves directly address the various problems that arise in the social order.

This discussion of employment naturally leads to a discussion of wages. "The key problem of social ethics in this case is that of *just remuneration* for work done" (no. 19). This, as we have seen, has been a major theme of papal social teaching since Leo XIII. John Paul reminds his readers of the connection between just wages and the family. "Just remuneration for the work of an adult who is responsible for a family means remuneration which will suffice for establishing and properly maintaining a family and for providing security for its future" (no. 19). This can be done either by means of "what is called a *family wage*—that is, a single salary given to the head of the family for his work, sufficient for the needs of the family without the other spouse having to take up gainful employment outside the home"—or by "family allowances or grants," which are common in many European countries. Such arrangements are a way a society can ensure that mothers are not forced to leave the home to take up paid work, something that is "wrong from the point of view of the good of society and of the family when it contradicts or hinders [the] primary goals of the mission of a mother" (no. 19).

Then the pope turns his attention to one important and practical way of securing many rights for workers: unions. Many previous popes had, of course, discussed and defended labor unions. Pius XI, for example, had complained about Catholic industrialists who were "hostile to a labor movement that We Ourselves recommended."[9] St. John Paul points out that it is false to say that "unions are no more than a reflection of the 'class' struggle" (no. 20). Rather, they are a necessary type of organization, "especially in modern industrialized societies" (ibid.). Unions are an example of the way work "first and foremost unites people" and of its "power to build a community" (ibid.). The pontiff then

8 "The gift of authority is from God, and is, as it were, a participation of the highest of all sovereignties; and it should be exercised as the power of God is exercised—with a fatherly solicitude which not only guides the whole but reaches to details as well." Leo XIII, *Rerum Novarum*, no. 35.

9 *Divini Redemptoris*, no. 50.

immediately makes a statement, which to anyone familiar with the tradition of Catholic social thought is a clear call for the establishment of the occupational groups so strongly called for by Pius XI and Pius XII: "In the final analysis, both those who work and those who manage the means of production or who own them must in some way be united in this community" (ibid.).

St. John Paul II brings *Laborem Exercens* to a close with some reflections on the spirituality of work. He insists especially on human work as a sharing in the activity of God the Creator, and quotes St. Paul's words, "whatever your task, work heartily, as serving the Lord and not men, knowing that from the Lord you will receive the inheritance as your reward" (Colossians 3:23–24). We realize, then, that it is the subject of work, the human person, who will live forever, either with God or without Him, and that the eternal aspects of our work will, in the end, be more important than the economic products that we create. Nonetheless, by a kind of paradox, in part by doing our work here well we can attain that eternal life which God himself invites us to share.

Just a few years after *Laborem Exercens*, on December 30, 1987, John Paul II issued the second of his social encyclicals, *Sollicitudo Rei Socialis*. Unlike most of the social encyclicals, which were published on an anniversary of Leo XIII's *Rerum Novarum*, *Sollicitudo* was issued to commemorate the twentieth anniversary of Paul VI's *Populorum Progressio*. In fact, John Paul states that he desires "to pay homage to this historic document of Paul VI" (no. 3) and "to extend the impact of that message by bringing it to bear…upon the present historical moment…" (no. 4). Not surprisingly, the Holy Father devotes the first part of *Sollicitudo* to a discussion of Paul VI's encyclical. He points out that *Populorum Progressio* brought out the "worldwide dimension" (no. 9) of the social question more clearly than any previous papal document. That encyclical had been devoted to the "development" or *progressio* of the peoples of the world, not merely to development conceived as an accumulation of goods, but as promoting "the good of every man and of the whole man."[10] Now in his own document, John Paul proposes "to develop the teaching of Paul VI's Encyclical…" (no. 11).

The entire context and background of all that the pontiff writes here consists in the fact that Paul VI's *"hopes for development…*today appear

10 *Populorum Progressio*, no. 14.

very far from being realized" (no. 12). In other words, the application of Catholic social teaching to the whole world and to relationships between nations that Paul VI called for with such urgency for the most part had not taken place. John Paul, then, devotes his encyclical to various reflections and comments on the situation twenty years after *Populorum Progressio*.

First, the Holy Father notes "the persistence and often the widening of the *gap* between the areas of the so-called developed North and the developing South" (no. 14). He instances also various oppressions and exploitations that were characteristic at the time of his writing. John Paul naturally is concerned with these injustices and the consequent poverty that exists in much of the world. His reflections on them, however, are far from simplistic, and his prescriptions and suggestions are based on a comprehensive view of things. For example, in a passage that anticipates his third social encyclical, *Centesimus Annus*, John Paul laments that "*the right of economic initiative* is often suppressed" (no. 15). He is clearly thinking here of the Communist countries, and speaks of the resulting "passivity, dependence and submission to the bureaucratic apparatus..." (ibid.). But the pope looks beyond the economic or social surface toward what must be the basis of every economic and social system—man himself. For he notes that in such a regime "*the creative subjectivity of the citizen*" (ibid.) is destroyed. Thus he links the socio-economic arrangements with man, the subject of work and of the economy, a matter discussed at length in *Laborem Exercens*. In evaluating the justice of any social system, its effects on man must always be the first thing looked at.

Moreover, he is far from exempting the developing nations themselves from a share in the blame for the present state of things.

> Responsibility for this deterioration [in conditions] is due to various causes. Notable among them are undoubtedly grave instances of omissions on the part of the developing nations themselves, and especially on the part of those holding economic and political power. (no. 16)

One can recall instances, for example, when the money loaned or given to developing countries was spent to benefit those in power instead of being used to improve conditions for the nation as a whole. Of course, this does not exempt from blame those in the rich countries who, by commission or omission, have contributed to the present condition of things.

Although mankind may not be developing according to the plan of God and the prescriptions of the Church, the interdependence of nations and peoples is nonetheless a reality. But when "this interdependence is separated from its ethical requirements, it has *disastrous consequences* for the weakest" (no. 17). When two or more countries of unequal economic strength make agreements for free trade, for example, can we assume that justice will arise spontaneously? To do so would be to ignore the explicit teaching of not only John Paul, but of Leo XIII and Pius XI, who both taught that justice could easily be violated in agreements in which the strong and powerful were able to dictate terms to the weak.[11]

In view of the many ways in which the true *progressio* of peoples has gone awry, the Holy Father repeats what has been the explicit judgment of the Magisterium since at least Leo XIII, that "the Church's social doctrine adopts a critical attitude towards both liberal capitalism and Marxist collectivism" (no. 21). And it is further the case that the political blocs of both East and West, which are based on these two social systems, are guilty of faults that have affected the developing world.

> Each of the two *blocs* harbors in its own way a tendency toward *imperialism*, as it is usually called, or toward forms of neo-colonialism: an easy temptation to which they frequently succumb, as history, including recent history, teaches. (no. 22)

Because of the existence of these two politico-military blocs, "each with its own forms of propaganda and indoctrination, the *ideological opposition*" has become "a growing *military opposition*" (no. 20). Accordingly, the great number of weapons introduced into the poorer nations by these two blocs has contributed to violence and warfare — for example, in Afghanistan and Central America — long after the collapse of the Soviet Union. John Paul addresses the following words to those countries that possess the economic or military power to influence world events.

> It is timely to mention — and it is no exaggeration — that a leadership role among nations can only be justified by the possibility and willingness to contribute widely and generously to the common good. (no. 23)

---

11 See *Rerum Novarum*, no. 45; *Quadragesimo Anno*, nos. 105–8, 132–33.

Then the pope includes a warning about "*systematic campaigns* against birth" that are often "the result of pressure and financing coming from abroad, and in some cases they are made a condition for the granting of financial and economic aid and assistance" (no. 25), a practice that continues to the present day.

Although nations and peoples are interdependent, this need not result in imperialism and exploitation.

> At the same time, in a world divided and beset by every type of conflict, the *conviction* is growing of a radical *interdependence* and consequently of the need for a solidarity which will take up interdependence and transfer it to the moral plane. (no. 26)

In other words, the physical fact of interdependence, or what we now call globalization, demands a corresponding moral fact of human solidarity. Just as Our Lord commands us to love our neighbors, nations must behave toward their neighbors with that same charity. Just because men form political communities with others does not relieve them of the duty to obey God's commandments.

The false idea of development, the notion that it consists in "the *mere accumulation* of goods and services" (no. 28), leads not only to injustices between nations but also to evils within even the rich nations.

> This is the so-called civilization of "consumption" or "consumerism," which involves so much "throwing-away" and "waste." An object already owned but now superseded by something better is discarded, with no thought of its possible lasting value in itself, nor of some other human being who is poorer. (no. 28)

St. John Paul goes on to say:

> To "have" objects and goods does not in itself perfect the human subject, unless it contributes to the maturing and enrichment of that subject's "being," that is to say unless it contributes to the realization of the human vocation as such. (ibid.)

He sums up this Christian conception of development with a phrase he used on many other occasions, the "civilization of love."

> In other words, true development must be based on the *love of God and neighbor*, and must help to promote the relationships between individuals and society. This is the "civilization of love" of which Paul VI often spoke. (no. 33)

Moreover, the desire to have more and more goods cannot be justified by an appeal to the commandment of God to "subdue the earth."

> The dominion granted to man by the Creator is not an absolute power, nor can one speak of a freedom to "use and misuse," or to dispose of things as one pleases. The limitation imposed from the beginning by the Creator himself and expressed symbolically by the prohibition not to "eat of the fruit of the tree" shows clearly enough that, when it comes to the natural world, we are subject not only to biological laws but also to moral ones, which cannot be violated with impunity. (no. 34)

In the fifth chapter of the encyclical, John Paul II considers why, from a moral point of view, "there has been no development—or very little, irregular, or even contradictory development…" (no. 35). He mentions again the two political blocs, each with its false approach, the one having an "*all-consuming desire for profit*," the other, "*the thirst for power*, with the intention of imposing one's will upon others." In each case, the pope continues, "one can add the expression: 'at any price'" (no. 37).

The Church is able to discern the obstacles to creating a civilization of justice and charity, but, as Pius XI also had insisted,[12] she "does not have *technical solutions* to offer for the problem of underdevelopment as such…" (no. 41). Social doctrine "belongs to the field, not of *ideology*, but of *theology* and particularly of moral theology. The teaching and spreading of her social doctrine are part of the Church's evangelizing mission" (ibid.).

The pope makes it clear again that each nation is ultimately the producer of its own development, and cannot passively await assistance from richer nations.

> Development demands above all a spirit of initiative on the part of the countries which need it. Each of them must act in accordance

---

12 *Quadragesimo Anno*, nos. 41–42.

with its own responsibilities, *not expecting everything* from the more favored countries, and acting in collaboration with others in the same situation. Each must discover and use to the best advantage its *own area of freedom*. Each must make itself capable of initiatives responding to its own needs as a society. (no. 44)

Although the "Church well knows that *no temporal achievement* is to be identified with the Kingdom of God" (no. 48), the corporal works of mercy are rooted in the New Testament,[13] and are part of the duty of Christians. For this reason Paul VI and John Paul II speak of development as a means of succoring our brethren throughout the world.

At the conclusion of this encyclical, the Holy Father entrusts the social situation of the world to the safeguard of the Blessed Virgin Mary (no. 49). He reminds us that the first miracle worked by Jesus Christ, that of providing wine to the wedding feast at Cana, was done at her request and intercession. "Her maternal concern extends to the *personal* and *social* aspects of people's life on earth" (ibid.). With this, he confides everything in his encyclical to Our Lady, in the presence of the Blessed Trinity. He concludes by implicitly recalling the great truth expressed by St. Paul, that God will renew all things in Christ, "things in heaven and things on earth" (Ephesians 1:10). Thus when we take part in the work of true development, we are aiding in that renewal, and making the world a more worthy offering to the Sacred Heart of our Redeemer.

---

13 See, for example, Matthew 25:31–46; Luke 1:53; Romans 15:26–27; I Corinthians 16:1–3; and James 2:14–17.

FIVE

John Paul II,
Centesimus Annus

S T. JOHN PAUL II WROTE HIS LAST SOCIAL ENCYCLICAL, *Centesimus Annus*, to commemorate the hundredth anniversary of *Rerum Novarum*, and issued it on May 1, 1991. In some quarters *Centesimus* was hailed as a new direction in papal social teaching, and even as a repudiation of past doctrine. However, as we will see, this was not at all the case, nor could it have been.[1] But because this charge has been widely made, I will devote much of this chapter to showing the continuity of *Centesimus* with the prior social doctrine of the Church.[2]

Centesimus appeared shortly after the startling fall of Communist regimes in eastern Europe and the Soviet Union. And even the Asian Communist countries, with the exception of North Korea, were modifying

---

1 Today and indeed since the conclusion of the Second Vatican Council the concept of development of doctrine has been bandied about in order to justify doctrinal *changes*, that is, the actual abandonment of prior teaching in favor of something new. But it is hard to see how such a thing could happen. In the first place, Cardinal Newman, who introduced the idea of doctrinal development into theology in his *Essay on the Development of Christian Doctrine* (1845), had no such concept of it. He rather wrote that "true development...is of a *tendency conservative* of what has gone before it." True development of doctrine does not contradict what came before, but rather unfolds truths half hidden or not clearly discerned in the earlier doctrinal statements. Similarly, the First Vatican Council taught that the "meaning of the sacred dogmas is perpetually to be retained which our holy Mother the Church has once declared; nor is that meaning ever to be departed from, under the pretence or pretext of a deeper comprehension of them" (Constitution *Dei Filius*).

It is evolutionary ideas, derived from biology, that have influenced theology here. For it is held, of course, that in biology one type of organism can actually, over time, become something different, something which bears only slight traces of its original ancestral species. Clearly if such a thing could occur in theology, no point of Catholic doctrine could be regarded as settled.

2 See also Appendix II, which reproduces my article, "What Does *Centesimus Annus* Really Teach?" Just as some have erected the Second Vatican Council into a "super council" which was held to negate everything that came before, so some erected *Centesimus* into a "super social encyclical," likewise seen as negating previous social doctrine. The absurdity of both claims should be obvious.

their economies to adopt many of the institutions of the capitalist West, a process that has continued since that time. As a result, Pope John Paul saw the need to give moral guidance to this new and unexpected situation that many thought to be a vindication of the Western economic system, which needed no correction — just celebration. In addition, as a former resident of socialist and totalitarian Poland, John Paul was familiar with the heavy, and inefficient, hand of centralized state planning, with its lack of freedom for private economic initiatives. In chapters three and five of the encyclical, one can see his preoccupation with the absence of freedom that characterized such regimes — thus his good words, even praise, for open economies. But such praise is always qualified. For John Paul is at pains to point out that freedom, including economic freedom, must be rooted in the truth, and as a result he is clear that economic activity must be circumscribed by a legal order that points it toward justice and the common good.[3] We will see how often St. John Paul returns to this theme.

Centesimus Annus opens with a brief introduction followed by six chapters. In the introduction John Paul invites his readers to look again at *Rerum Novarum* "in order to discover anew the richness of the fundamental principles which it formulated…" (no. 3). Moreover, he states that in *Centesimus* he "seeks to show the fruitfulness of the principles enunciated by Leo XIII, which belong to the Church's doctrinal patrimony and, as such, involve the exercise of her teaching authority" (ibid.). Thus, far from seeking to set a new course for social doctrine, the pontiff roots his own teaching firmly in that of Pope Leo, the continuing validity of which he affirms.

With this introduction, he devotes the first chapter to *Rerum Novarum*. He notes the "radical changes which had taken place in the political, economic and social fields" at the time of that encyclical. As a result of these economic changes, labor had become

> a commodity to be freely bought and sold on the market, its price determined by the law of supply and demand, without taking into account the bare minimum required for the support of the individual and his family. (no. 4)

St. John Paul describes this situation as a "grave injustice" (ibid.) and he summarizes some of the points Leo XIII made in response. He notes that

---

3 See especially nos. 4, 11, 15, 17, 34, 36, 42, 48 and 58.

Leo "affirmed the fundamental rights of workers" as well as the right to private property, noting that the earlier pontiff had been "well aware that private property is not an absolute value." Leo had also proclaimed the "necessary complementary principles, such as the *universal destination of the earth's goods*" (no. 6). Then Pope John Paul discusses *Rerum Novarum*'s vindication of the right "to form private associations. This means above all *the right to establish professional associations* of employers and workers, or of workers alone." And in this human right "we find the reason for the Church's defense and approval of the establishment of what are commonly called trade unions...because the right of association is a natural right of the human being" (no. 7).

Next the Holy Father mentions other rights of the worker that had been specified by Pope Leo. These include rights to reasonable working hours and periods of rest, to a safe workplace, and to a just wage. Indeed, John Paul affirms: "A workman's wages should be sufficient to enable him to support himself, his wife and his children." And immediately he quotes Leo XIII: "If through necessity or fear of a worse evil the workman accepts harder conditions because an employer or contractor will afford no better, he is made the victim of force and injustice" (no. 8). John Paul goes on to say:

> Would that these words, written at a time when what has been called "unbridled capitalism" was pressing forward, should not have to be repeated today with the same severity. Unfortunately, even today one finds instances of contracts between employers and employees which lack reference to the most elementary justice regarding the employment of children or women, working hours, the hygienic conditions of the workplace and fair pay.... (ibid.)

John Paul speaks of Leo XIII's discussion of two erroneous socio-political theories, socialism and liberalism. And here I must again remind the reader that liberalism, as used in the papal social encyclicals, does not mean what it means in the United States. It has the European meaning, which approaches what we would call libertarianism, or, in economic matters, the "unbridled capitalism" that supports a market economy free of all or most legal or regulatory restraints. Socialism, by and large, is no longer a temptation to most people, but free-market liberalism is currently enjoying a resurgence, as Paul VI had observed as early as 1971. John Paul reminds his readers that

> the State has the duty of watching over the common good and of
> ensuring that every sector of social life, not excluding the economic
> one, contributes to achieving that good, while respecting the rightful
> autonomy of each sector. (no. 11)

This is in contrast to the free-market liberal or libertarian view of the
state, which sees the state as merely enforcing peace and preventing fraud,
and posits that market forces will always tend toward the common good.
Indeed, if this contrast between Catholic teaching and liberal dogma is
fully grasped, it will be found to contain a profound commentary on
modern society and modern economics.

I cannot leave this first chapter of *Centesimus* without noting the Holy
Father's statements that "to spread her social doctrine pertains to the
Church's evangelizing mission and is an essential part of the Christian
message" and that the "'new evangelization' which the modern world
urgently needs...must include among its essential elements *a proclamation
of the Church's social doctrine*" (no. 5).

We can see by looking at the first chapter of John Paul's encyclical that
far from weakening the doctrine of his predecessors, the Holy Father is
determined to reaffirm and apply it to today. Exactly how he does this we
shall see in the remainder of our discussion.

John Paul begins the second chapter of *Centesimus* with an analysis
of the world situation since *Rerum Novarum*, including the situation of
today. First, the pontiff speaks of socialism, which in Leo XIII's time was
"still only a social philosophy, and not yet a fully structured movement,"
let alone in control of "a strong and powerful State..." (no. 12). But Pope
Leo divined the evils of socialism quite clearly. Moreover, as Pius XI had
also pointed out,[4] and as John Paul points out now, "the fundamental
error of socialism is anthropological in nature" (no. 13). That is, since
socialism conceives of man wrongly, it necessarily conceives of the state
and society wrongly, and in turn, conceives of the economy wrongly.
And this wrong conception of man is the notion that the human person
is merely "an element, a molecule within the social organism, so that the
good of the individual is completely subordinated to the functioning of
the socio-economic mechanism" (ibid.). Socialism also ignores man's
power of free choice and "the unique and exclusive responsibility which

---

4 *Quadragesimo Anno*, nos. 117–119.

he exercises in the face of good or evil" (ibid.). Ultimately these errors are rooted in socialism's atheism, which "deprives the person of his foundation, and consequently leads to a reorganization of the social order without reference to the person's dignity and responsibility" (ibid.).

If the socialist errors about God and man lead to an evil socio-economic system, "from the Christian vision of the human person there necessarily follows a correct picture of society" (ibid.). That is, if we correctly perceive the truth about God and man, we will correctly perceive the truth about society, including the economic system. The pope immediately continues by pointing out that atheism is not confined just to the socialists.

> The atheism of which we are speaking is also closely connected with the rationalism of the Enlightenment, which views human and social reality in a mechanistic way. Thus there is a denial of the supreme insight concerning man's true greatness, his transcendence in respect to earthly realities...and, above all, the need for salvation.... (ibid.)

The "mechanistic" viewpoint that John Paul II is criticizing here is, of course, that of the founders of modern economic and capitalistic doctrine, such as the Physiocrats in France and Adam Smith in Scotland. This suggests that at bottom the liberal capitalism of the Western world is founded on atheism in a way similar to socialism. This seems to be confirmed, as we will see below, when the pope speaks of the post-World War II economies of Europe and America.[5] In any case, John Paul's repeated statements that the economic order requires a legal framework to point the market toward the common good shows that he by no means accepts the tradition of the self-regulating market stemming from Enlightenment rationalism.

The pontiff next takes up this very theme, the need for a "juridical framework within which economic affairs are to be conducted..." (no. 15). That is, although economic activity must have a "legitimate sphere of autonomy," at the same time it must respect certain necessities of the human person, and there must be some means to guarantee that this

---

5 In May of 1949, during the reign of Pius XII, the Vatican's newspaper, *L'Osservatore Romano*, carried an editorial in which it stated that "communism...as an economic system, does not run counter to the nature of Christian doctrine as strongly as capitalism." The article said that capitalism "is atheistic in its structure; gold is its God." The editorial was written by the paper's editor-in-chief, Count Giuseppe Dalla Torre. For an account of this article, see *The New York Times*, Sunday May 8, 1949, 8.

will be done. For example, "society and the State must ensure wage levels adequate for the maintenance of the worker and his family" and "working hours" must be such as not to oppress the worker (ibid.). Both Leo XIII and Pius XI had made the same points in their social encyclicals. Here John Paul mentions not only the state's role in achieving these goods for the worker, but also the "decisive" role of unions in this as well.

Next the pontiff makes two points that should give pause to many Western critics of communism. We are apt to contrast our social system with communism by pointing out the freedom that we have and the lack of freedom that existed under Marxism. We even called ourselves the *Free World*, not the Just World or the Godly World. John Paul describes here the root error related to freedom, namely "an understanding of human freedom which detaches it from obedience to the truth... which leads to an unbridled affirmation of self-interest and which refuses to be limited by any demand of justice" (no. 17). If we recall that the economic model which affirms the individual's unlimited self-interest has often been championed as the alternative to communism, this passage should make us think twice about the implications of this.

Then the pope writes of the situation after World War II, of the Marxist totalitarian states and alternatives proposed against communism. First he speaks of what was

> in some countries... a positive effort to rebuild a democratic society inspired by social justice, so as to deprive Communism of the revolutionary potential represented by masses of people subjected to exploitation and oppression. In general, such attempts endeavor to preserve free market mechanisms, ensuring, by means of a stable currency and the harmony of social relations, the conditions for steady and healthy economic growth.... At the same time, these attempts try to avoid making market mechanisms the only point of reference for social life, and they tend to subject them to public control which upholds the principle of the common destination of material goods. In this context, an abundance of work opportunities, a solid system of social security and professional training, the freedom to join trade unions and the effective action of unions... are meant to deliver work from the mere condition of "a commodity," and to guarantee its dignity. (no. 19)

This seems to be a description of the West German social market economy, as it is sometimes called, a system of "codetermination" in which unions and management see themselves as partners and unions have a considerable voice in the management of firms.[6] Another alternative of that era is also described by the pope, one that seems to embody the atheism that is "closely connected with the rationalism of the Enlightenment." This is

> the affluent society or the consumer society [*in commodorum societate... vel in rerum consumptionis societate*]. It seeks to defeat Marxism on the level of pure materialism by showing how a free-market society can achieve a greater satisfaction of material human needs than Communism, while equally excluding spiritual values. In reality, while on the one hand it is true that this social model shows the failure of Marxism to contribute to a humane and better society, on the other hand, insofar as it denies an autonomous existence and value to morality, law, culture and religion, it agrees with Marxism, in the sense that it totally reduces man to the sphere of economics and the satisfaction of material needs. (no. 19)

Where was this "affluent society" or "consumer society" located? Americans have often boasted of our affluence and surely we must recognize that the pontiff is speaking primarily of us. It is our society that has tried to surpass communism on a purely material level "while equally excluding spiritual values." And although we have succeeded well enough at that, surely there is more to living than possessing an abundance of things. As Our Lord said, "a man's life does not consist in the abundance of his possessions" (Luke 12:15).

In the next chapter of the encyclical, chapter three, John Paul II discusses the events of the year 1989, the year that saw the fall of most of

---

6 Codetermination, an organized system of cooperation between workers and management, was established in Germany in 1951. It can be described as follows:

"Employers' associations and trade unions do not see themselves as opponents but as partners in an agreement that forms the basis of the economic development of the country. Each side is fully aware that it is dependent upon the other. Both know that at the end of negotiations, agreement must be reached. Furthermore, both sides affirm their responsibility for finding solutions to existing social problems. This results in a basic consensus that is not destroyed by occasional industrial disputes. For this reason, employers' organizations and trade unions in Germany are usually referred to as *social partners*."

Under codetermination, the chief board of a German industrial concern is comprised of "an equal number of shareholders' representatives and employees' representatives...." Uwe Liebig, "Dialogue Instead of Confrontation: the German System," *Canada–U.S. Outlook*, 3, no. 4 (1993): 56–57.

the Communist governments throughout eastern Europe. The pope identifies and discusses three reasons for the fall of these regimes. The first is "the violation of the rights of workers." He mentions, of course, the Solidarity movement in his native Poland, where the workers, on account of "a hard, lived experience of work and of oppression…recovered and… rediscovered the content and principles of the Church's social doctrine" (no. 23). The experience of living and working in the "workers' paradise" of communism rightly convinced them of the injustices to which they were subjected.

Second, the pontiff mentions the "inefficiency of the economic system," which is more than the inability to produce sufficient goods, but involves a restriction of human freedom. Connected to this, he adds, is communism's understanding of "the human person on the basis of economics alone," a practice which is basic to Marxist philosophy. For a "human being is understood in a more complete way when situated within the sphere of culture through language, history, and the position one takes towards the fundamental events of life…" (no. 24). In other words, we are more than producing and consuming beings — even the irrational animals do that. What makes us distinctly human is a complex of factors revolving around a culture, and no economic system can rightly ignore that complex of factors.

Third, the Holy Father specifies "the spiritual void brought about by atheism" as in fact the principal cause of communism's fall. This had "deprived the younger generations of a sense of direction," although in some cases this ultimately brought them to Christ, "as the existentially adequate response to the desire in every human heart for goodness, truth and life" (no. 24).

This fact shows the insufficiency of merely political or social systems to fulfill man's longings. In making use of merely political means to bring about justice and peace, politics can become a "'secular religion' which operates under the illusion of creating paradise in this world" (no. 25). But the Kingdom of God, which is in but not *of* this world, "throws light on the order of human society" (ibid.). In this light we can better see what is needed for a true rebuilding of human society. The Holy Father touches on several other topics as he closes this chapter, including the effort to reconstruct Europe after the fall of communism, and the fact that aid for this project "must not lead to a slackening of efforts to sustain and assist the countries of the Third World…" (28). And finally, the pope, echoing

Paul VI's encyclical *Populorum Progressio*, reminds us that "development must not be understood solely in economic terms, but in a way that is fully human" (no. 29). Most importantly, the "apex of development is the exercise of the right and duty to seek God, to know him and to live in accordance with that knowledge" (ibid.).

The fourth and longest chapter of *Centesimus Annus* concerns the twin truths of the right to private property, and at the same time, of the universal destination of material goods. This is the same truth that Leo XIII stated when he said: "The earth, though divided among private owners, ceases not thereby to minister to the needs of all."[7] That is, the reason why God instituted the private ownership of property among men is not to exclude anyone from his share of the earth's bounty, but rather to make possible the orderly and peaceful provision of sufficient goods for all. Thus private property is simply a *means* to an end; it is not an end in itself, "not an absolute value," as John Paul had earlier noted. Though it is surely a means consonant with human nature, and therefore it cannot be abrogated by human law, it is nevertheless subordinate to its end, and thus can be regulated so as to better attain that end, as Pius XI had already taught.[8] Accordingly, the chief matter that the Holy Father takes up in this chapter is what he calls "the legitimacy of private ownership, as well as the limits which are imposed on it" (no. 30). John Paul states therefore that

> God gave the earth to the whole human race for the sustenance of all its members, ... [but] the earth does not yield its fruits without a particular human response to God's gift, that is to say, without work. (no. 31)

As a result, the pontiff points out, not only the earth (in the sense of land) but also human skill and ability (including the ability to organize and direct) are increasingly important parts of the reaping of the earth's fruits. "Indeed, besides the earth, humankind's principal resource is *the person himself*" (no. 32). This leads the pope to state one of the first of his conclusions that have led some people to suppose that *Centesimus* somehow represents a break with all prior papal social teaching. The pope's statement is this: "The modern *business economy* has positive aspects. Its basis is human freedom exercised in the economic field, just

---

7 *Rerum Novarum*, no. 8.
8 *Quadragesimo Anno*, nos. 48 and 49.

as it is exercised in many other fields" (ibid.). But in this passage, as in others, there is continuity with earlier social teaching; they do not represent any kind of break with his predecessors' doctrine. Let us look at one of the most explicit of these statements: "It would appear that, on the level of individual nations and of international relations, *the free market* is the most efficient instrument for utilizing resources and effectively responding to needs" (no. 34). But then, beginning with the very next sentence, the pontiff adds:

> But this is true only for those needs which are "solvent," insofar as they are endowed with purchasing power, and for those resources which are "marketable," insofar as they are capable of obtaining a satisfactory price. But there are many human needs which find no place on the market. It is a strict duty of justice and truth not to allow fundamental human needs to remain unsatisfied, and not to allow those burdened by such needs to perish.... Even prior to the logic of a fair exchange of goods and the forms of justice appropriate to it, there exists *something which is due to the person because he is a person*, by reason of his lofty dignity.

This is essentially the same as Pius XI's teaching in *Quadragesimo Anno* (no. 88) that "free competition...though justified and quite useful within certain limits, cannot be an adequate controlling principle in economic affairs." For if "there are many human needs which find no place in the market," and if it is "a strict duty of justice and truth not to allow fundamental human needs to remain unsatisfied," then the free market cannot be the controlling principle of the economy, however useful it might be at times. Nor is it correct to say that the needs "which find no place on the market" might be things such as love or beauty or other intangible items. For the pontiff says that it is "a strict duty of justice and truth" to meet these needs, so it is obvious he is speaking of tangible and material things. It appears John Paul is addressing the imperative that those whose "human needs...find no place on the market," whether because of their poverty or for some other reason, still must have those needs met, because "there exists *something which is due*" to them simply because they are human beings. In fact, we see this principle reiterated throughout this encyclical in various ways, for example, in the affirmation of the necessity for a just wage.

Immediately after this the pope speaks of certain Third World nations where even the prescriptions of *Rerum Novarum* have not yet been realized. As a help in realizing the mandates of Pope Leo, John Paul instances the work of labor unions. It is again obvious that the Holy Father does not simply appeal to the workings of the free market to correct the situations he cites. For the market has had more than a hundred years to bring about justice and human dignity. But as all the popes have recognized, the market cannot on its own do so, without intervention, for, as John Paul says in the next section, it is necessary "that the market be appropriately controlled by the forces of society and by the State, so as to guarantee that the basic needs of the whole of society are satisfied" (no. 35).

We see, then, that John Paul II does have praise, within limits, for the "modern business economy." But lest it be thought that the Church has unequivocally embraced a kind of modified capitalism, the pope goes out of his way to say that "it is unacceptable to say that the defeat of so-called 'Real Socialism' leaves capitalism as the only model of economic organization" (no. 35). By "Real Socialism" he means, of course, Marxist socialism or communism. Therefore whether one regards oneself as an adherent of capitalism or not, the duties of justice and charity cataloged here and in the other encyclicals still must be carried out in any economic system that can be acceptable to a Catholic.

The supreme pontiff next turns his attention to the "specific problems and threats emerging within the more advanced economies..." (no. 36). And first he speaks of the increasing quantity of goods and the desire "for an existence which is qualitatively more satisfying..." (ibid.). In itself this is not wrong, he states, but there are dangers connected with it. John Paul points out that the "manner in which new needs arise and are defined is always marked by a more or less appropriate concept of the human person and of the person's true good" (ibid.). If our culture creates a "need" to have a new car, new clothes, and new appliances every year, it is proposing a concept of man and of what is good for man. It is defining us by our possessions. "A given culture reveals its overall understanding of life through the choices it makes in production and consumption" (ibid.). Thus "*a great deal of educational and cultural work* is urgently needed" in order to form people to make responsible choices. The pope notes here the duty of the media in "the formation of a strong sense of responsibility" among people, and, significantly, the need for "intervention by public authorities" (ibid.).

The concept of man that defines him primarily as a consumer and that assumes he needs more and more goods to make him happy presupposes

> a style of life which is presumed to be better when it is directed toward 'having' rather than 'being,' and which wants to have more, not in order to be more but in order to spend life in enjoyment as an end in itself. (ibid.)

But this is wrong.

> It is therefore necessary to create lifestyles in which the quest for truth, beauty, goodness and communion with others for the sake of common growth are the factors which determine consumer choices, savings and investments. (ibid.)

Another of the "problems and threats emerging within the more advanced economies" is the destruction of the physical environment. John Paul devotes the next section to this point. He succinctly sums up the problem this way: "In their desire to have and to enjoy rather than to be and to grow, people consume the resources of the earth and their own lives in an excessive and disordered way." Because this frenzied consumerism is rooted in a false notion of man, as we saw above, "the senseless destruction of the natural environment" is likewise rooted in

> an anthropological error, which unfortunately is widespread in our day.... In all this, one notes first the poverty or narrowness of the human outlook, motivated as people are by a desire to possess things rather than to relate to the truth.... (no. 37)

But it is not only "the irrational destruction of the natural environment" that concerns the pontiff, but also "the more serious destruction of the *human environment...*" (no. 38) — that is, "*the moral conditions for an authentic 'human ecology'*" (ibid.). St. John Paul mentions under this head "the social structure in which one lives...the education one has received," the problem of urbanization, but most especially, the family, which is the

> first and fundamental structure for "human ecology"... in which [one] receives his first formative ideas about truth and goodness,

and learns what it means to love and to be loved, and thus what it
actually means to be a person. (no. 39)

In this connection the Holy Father specifies that he is speaking of a family
"founded on marriage" and criticizes tendencies that discourage people
from committing themselves to a stable marriage and from having children. He mentions even more extreme attacks on life, such as abortion
and "systematic anti-childbearing campaigns."

In the next section the pope again discusses the state's tasks with regard
to the

> preservation of common goods such as the natural and human
> environments, which cannot be safeguarded simply by market
> forces. Just as in the time of primitive capitalism the State had the
> duty of defending the basic rights of workers, so now, with the new
> capitalism, the State and all of society have the duty of *defending*
> *those collective goods* which, among others, constitute the essential
> framework for the legitimate pursuit of personal goals on the part
> of each individual. (no. 40)

And in the very next paragraph he continues: "Here we find a new limit
on the market: there are collective and qualitative needs that cannot be
satisfied by market mechanisms. There are important human needs which
escape its logic." It should be clear from these, as well as from other passages
I have quoted from *Centesimus Annus*, that far from endorsing free-market capitalism, John Paul II devotes much space to reiterating Catholic
teaching, which has always deemed the market as a less than trustworthy
arbiter of a just economy or social order. Every social encyclical, as well
as many addresses of Pope Pius XII, has made it clear that Catholic moral
teaching cannot accept the market according to its own logic — that is,
according to a logic that sees the market and market solutions as able to
take care of all or most socio-economic difficulties and needs. Any Catholic
who wishes to remain orthodox must come to terms with this repeated
teaching of the Magisterium.

In the next section John Paul II considers the concept of alienation, a
concept derived from Karl Marx. In *The German Ideology* Marx and Engels
characterize alienation as when "man's own deed becomes an alien power
opposed to him, which enslaves him instead of being controlled by him,"

because the social system forces a certain social and economic role upon him "from which he cannot escape."[9] John Paul, however, rightly calls this concept of alienation "mistaken and inadequate" (no. 41). Moreover, history has proven that the Marxist cure for alienation, the establishment of a communistic society, itself "rather increases it, adding to it a lack of basic necessities and economic inefficiency" (ibid.).

Nevertheless, alienation does exist in the capitalistic West, particularly

> in consumerism, when people are ensnared in a web of false and superficial gratifications rather than being helped to experience their personhood in an authentic and concrete way. Alienation is found also in work, when it is organized so as to ensure maximum returns and profits with no concern whether the worker, through his own labor, grows or diminishes as a person.... (ibid.)

Ultimately alienation is overcome only by the giving of oneself to the person of Jesus Christ. Further, a *society* can be alienated if it makes it harder for one to make this gift of self to both God and other human persons.

Following this, St. John Paul II returns to the question of the meaning and value of capitalism. He asks:

> Can it perhaps be said that, after the failure of Communism, capitalism is the victorious social system, and that capitalism should be the goal of the countries now making efforts to rebuild their economy and society? (no. 42)

John Paul's answer to his question is interesting and indicates how it is *things*, not *names*, that should be the object of our considerations. For he states that it basically depends on what one means by the word *capitalism*.

> If by "capitalism" is meant an economic system which recognizes the fundamental and positive role of business, the market, private property and the resulting responsibility for the means of production, as well as free human creativity in the economic sector, then the answer is certainly in the affirmative, even though it would perhaps be more appropriate to speak of a "business economy," "market economy" or

9 Karl Marx and Frederick Engels, *The German Ideology* (New York: International Publishers, 1970), 53.

simply "free economy." But if by "capitalism" is meant a system in which freedom in the economic sector is not circumscribed within a strong juridical framework which places it at the service of human freedom in its totality and sees it as a particular aspect of that freedom, the core of which is ethical and religious, then the reply is certainly negative. (no. 42)

This is similar to Pius XI's statement:

It is therefore very necessary that economic affairs be once more subjected to and governed by a true and effective guiding princi-ple.... To that end all the institutions of public and social life must be imbued with the spirit of justice, and this justice must above all be truly operative. It must build up a juridical and social order able to pervade all economic activity.[10]

In other words, although economic activity must not be shackled as it was in Communist countries, it must serve the common good, and there must be laws — that is, "a strong juridical framework" — to see that this does indeed happen. We have already seen numerous passages in this encyclical indicating the necessity of ordering economic activity according to juridical norms.

The next section, which begins with the statement, "the Church has no models to present," has led some to suppose that the Church has abandoned any hope of presenting an alternative system to socialism or capitalism. But the rest of the sentence explains the meaning:

Models that are real and truly effective can only arise within the framework of different historical situations, through the efforts of all those who responsibly confront concrete problems in all their... aspects.... For such a task the Church offers her social teaching as an *indispensable and ideal orientation*, a teaching which...recognizes the positive value of the market and of enterprise, but which...points out that these need to be oriented toward the common good. (no. 43)

Models, that is, concrete economic proposals and systems, must not be elaborated in the abstract or imposed from the top down, but must arise

10 *Quadragesimo Anno*, no. 88.

"within the framework of different historical situations," created by "those who responsibly confront concrete problems in all their…aspects." To those formulating such economic models, John Paul makes it clear that the Church's acceptance of a market economy depends on whether that economy truly serves the common good. Service to the common good cannot be left to chance or to the supposed automatic laws of the market, Adam Smith's "invisible hand." The state must be prepared to play its part in making such a service of man's true welfare a reality. *Centesimus* updates and applies Catholic social teaching to our times, and contrasts it with the Communist economies that had lately fallen throughout eastern Europe and the Soviet Union. This encyclical does develop the teaching of previous popes, but not in the sense of abandoning anything they taught, which is of course an impossibility. The pope approaches the regnant capitalism of our day in a friendly manner and points out its flaws and where it needs to improve, much as Pius XI discussed the economy of Fascist Italy in his encyclical.[11]

The next chapter of *Centesimus* deals with the theme of state and culture. John Paul opens it by an extended discussion of totalitarianism, pointing out its denial of truth and of the dignity of the human person. After discussing the flaws of Communist and other dictatorial states, the pope next turns his attention to democratic regimes. He first discusses abortion, which surely is as great an attack on the human person as was perpetrated by non-democratic governments. But he also speaks of "a crisis within democracies themselves, which seem at times to have lost the ability to make decisions aimed at the common good" (no. 47). He is referring to the tendency of democratic governments to be captives to special interest groups and of democratic politicians to support policies only to help themselves get reelected. "With time, such distortions of political conduct create distrust and apathy, with a subsequent decline in the political participation and civic spirit of the general population, which feels abused and disillusioned" (ibid.).

One phenomenon that has characterized many democratic states is the so-called welfare state, or as the Holy Father also calls it, the Social Assistance State. He is critical of its "excesses and abuses," such as

> a loss of human energies and an inordinate increase of public agen-
> cies, which are dominated more by bureaucratic ways of thinking

---

11 See *Quadragesimo Anno*, nos. 91–95.

than by concern for serving their clients, and which are accompanied by an enormous increase in spending. (no. 48)

He goes on to say that "it would appear that needs are best understood and satisfied by people who are closest to them and who act as neighbors to those in need" (ibid.). This sounds as if the pontiff were advocating entirely doing away with state assistance to the poor and needy. But this is not so, for in the next section he writes:

> It can happen, however, that when a family does decide to live up fully to its vocation, it finds itself without the necessary support from the State and without sufficient resources. It is urgent therefore to promote not only family policies, but also those social policies which have the family as their principal object, policies which assist the family by providing adequate resources and efficient means of support.... (no. 49)

The pope ends this chapter by reminding his readers that the Church supports the "adequate formation of a culture" since "the first and most important task is accomplished within the heart.... The Church promotes those aspects of human behavior which favor a true culture of peace..." (no. 51). He recalls the many times he and his predecessors have called for peace, and for the true development of nations, the lack of which can be a barrier to peace. Moreover, the promotion of such development

> may mean making important changes in established lifestyles, in order to limit the waste of environmental and human resources, thus enabling every individual and all the peoples of the earth to have a sufficient share of those resources. (no. 52)

These words should be matter for an examination of conscience for us as individuals, as well as for our societies and nations collectively.

The last chapter of *Centesimus* is called "The Person Is the Way of the Church," and John Paul begins by saying that in her social teaching the Church's "*care and responsibility*" has been "for the human person" (no. 53), the concrete individual person. But since "a person's true identity is only fully revealed to him through faith," the Church's social doctrine is likewise rooted in the Gospel and "is aimed at helping everyone on the

path of salvation" (no. 54). Thus the Church is naturally eager to make this
doctrine widely known, which is part of "an evangelization which promotes
the whole human being" (no. 55). There are two additional reasons the
Holy Father cites for making her social teaching better known. First, the
former Communist countries "are experiencing a serious lack of direction
in the work of rebuilding." And second, "the Western countries, in turn,
run the risk of seeing [the collapse of communism] as a one-sided victory
of their own economic system, and thereby failing to make necessary
corrections in that system" (no. 56). This sentence by itself ought to be
enough to convince us that we misunderstand John Paul II if we think he
has endorsed our own economic system.

The pope then speaks of the necessity of Christians to live out social doctrine. "Today more than ever, the Church is aware that her social message
will gain credibility more immediately from the *witness of actions* than as
a result of its internal logic and consistency" (no. 57). In connection with
this, he repeats a point he made earlier (in both no. 36 and no. 52), that
"above all a change of lifestyles, of models of production and consumption, and of the established structures of power" (no. 58) is required. For
example, with increasing economic globalization, unless "this increasing
internationalization of the economy [is] accompanied by effective international agencies which will oversee and direct the economy to the common
good," something that is beyond the power of any single nation, "even if
it were the most powerful on earth" (ibid.), this global economy cannot
otherwise be directed toward the common good of mankind.

After a brief survey of the Church's constant concern with the human
person in her social teaching, John Paul II concludes *Centesimus*, invoking
Almighty God and the Blessed Virgin, who

> constantly remained beside Christ in his journey towards the human
> family and in its midst, and [who] goes before the Church on the pil-
> grimage of faith. May her maternal intercession accompany humanity
> towards the next millennium, in fidelity to him who "is the same
> yesterday and today and for ever," Jesus Christ our Lord.... (no. 62)

SIX

Benedict XVI and Francis

POPE BENEDICT XVI'S *CARITAS IN VERITATE* WAS ISSUED on June 29, 2009, and, as one might expect, continues and develops many of the themes that we have already seen in papal social documents. Indeed, more than once it appears that Pope Benedict wrote specifically to correct the misinterpretations, whether deliberate or not, of St. John Paul II's *Centesimus Annus*. And since Benedict's encyclical appeared in the midst of a worldwide economic downturn—what has sometimes been called the Great Recession—it touches on the economic difficulties of today and possible remedies for these difficulties.

Benedict begins his encyclical with an introduction that he largely devotes to the concept of *charity*. This is obviously an important theme of this letter, since it appears in the title itself. This might puzzle some, since the previous social encyclicals, especially those of Leo XIII and Pius XI, stressed more the virtue of *justice* in the economy, even if they did not neglect the necessary role of charity. Pius XI, for example, had written that "charity cannot take the place of justice unfairly withheld,"[1] and that "a 'charity' which deprives the workingman of the salary to which he has a strict title in justice is not charity at all, but only its empty name and hollow semblance."[2] How then are we to understand Pope Benedict's emphasis on charity? Pope Benedict makes it clear not only that he recognizes the necessary place of justice in the social doctrine of the Church, but that his teaching on this is the same as that of his predecessors. He states:

> *Charity goes beyond justice*, because to love is to give, to offer what is "mine" to the other; but it never lacks justice, which prompts us to give the other what is "his," what is due to him by reason of his being or his acting. I cannot "give" what is mine to the other, without first

1 *Quadragesimo Anno*, no. 137.
2 *Divini Redemptoris*, no. 49.

giving him what pertains to him in justice. If we love others with
charity, then first of all we are just towards them. Not only is justice
not extraneous to charity,…justice is inseparable from charity and
intrinsic to it. (no. 6)

Why then does he give such prominence to charity? Because "charity
is at the heart of the Church's social doctrine" (no. 2). Benedict reminds
us that "according to the teaching of Jesus, [charity] is the synthesis of the
entire Law" (ibid.), including thereby the commandments of justice itself.
Of course, previous popes had also spoken of charity, with "social charity"
being one of the key concepts of Pius XI.[3] But Pope Benedict reminds us
that "the more we strive to secure a common good corresponding to the
real needs of our neighbors, the more effectively we love them" (no. 7).
Thus, in a sense, charity or love is the motivating factor in working for
justice. "When animated by charity, commitment to the common good
has greater worth than a merely secular and political stand would have"
(ibid.). As Pius XI wrote:

> Now, in effecting this reform [of the economy], charity "which is the
> bond of perfection," must play a leading part. How completely deceived
> are those inconsiderate reformers, who, zealous only for commutative
> justice, proudly disdain the help of charity. Charity cannot take the
> place of justice unfairly withheld, but, even though a state of things
> be pictured in which every man receives at last all that is his due, a
> wide field will nevertheless remain open for charity. For justice alone,
> even though most faithfully observed, can remove indeed the cause of
> social strife, but can never bring about a union of hearts and minds.[4]

Thus it is wrong to emphasize justice at the expense of charity, or *vice versa*,
since "justice is inseparable from charity and intrinsic to it."

After these words on charity and justice Benedict XVI notes the purpose
of his encyclical, to commemorate Paul VI's encyclical, *Populorum Progressio*, "to pay tribute and to honor [his] memory…, revisiting his teachings
on *integral human development* and taking my place within the path that
they marked out, so as to apply them to the present moment" (no. 8).
John Paul II, in *Sollicitudo Rei Socialis*, had already issued an encyclical

---

3 See *Quadragesimo Anno*, nos. 88 and 137.
4 *Quadragesimo Anno*, no. 137.

commemorating *Populorum Progressio*. This shows how fundamental the two supreme pontiffs considered Paul VI's encyclical to be. Indeed, Pope Benedict notes his "conviction that *Populorum Progressio* deserves to be considered 'the *Rerum Novarum* of the present age,' shedding light upon humanity's journey toward unity" (ibid.). Since according to some publicists John Paul II's *Centesimus Annus* was the social encyclical that somehow negated everything in the past, Benedict's commemoration of Paul VI's *Populorum Progressio* — and by implication John Paul II's *Sollicitudo Rei Socialis* — ought to remind Catholics that the previous social documents of the Church's Magisterium have by no means been superseded by *Centesimus*. Benedict, however, makes this explicit. He writes:

> It is not a case of two typologies of social doctrine, one pre-conciliar and one post-conciliar, differing from one another: on the contrary, there is *a single teaching, consistent and at the same time ever new*. It is one thing to draw attention to the particular characteristics of one Encyclical or another, of the teaching of one Pope or another, but quite another to lose sight of the coherence of the overall doctrinal *corpus*. (no. 12)

This ought to put a stop to those whose partial and tendentious reading of *Centesimus Annus* leads/led them to claim that it alone constitutes the future of the Church's social doctrine.

After the introduction, *Caritas in Veritate* is divided into six chapters, each a loose grouping of topics around a common theme. The first chapter is entitled "The Message of *Populorum Progressio*," and reviews the contents and importance of that encyclical, as well as other social documents of Paul VI's reign. Benedict focuses on what he more than once calls "*integral human development*." *Populorum Progressio* dealt, of course, with the development, or progress, of peoples or nations, but more fundamentally with what actually constitutes authentic human development. Pope Benedict reflects on this question and draws attention to certain essential points. First, he notes that "*the whole Church... when she performs works of charity... is engaged in promoting integral human development*. She has a public role over and above her charitable and educational activities..." (no. 11). In other words, the Church's apostolate of charitable works, including education, must be understood as part of the fostering of "*integral human development*," the promotion of the good of the entire human person, individually and socially. When Benedict reviews several of Paul VI's other documents, including *Octogesima Adveniens*, *Humanae Vitae*, and *Evangelii Nuntiandi*, he shows how each, in its own way, is concerned with human development. *Evangelii Nuntiandi*, for example, the 1975 apostolic exhortation on evangelization, "is very closely linked with development" in that (quoting Paul VI) "evangelization would not be complete if it did not take account of the unceasing interplay of the Gospel and of man's concrete life, both personal and social." In other words, instead of seeing the various Christian apostolates — preaching the Gospel, doing corporal works of mercy, educating, promoting economic justice — as so many separate responses to the commandments of God and the Church, we should see them as all connected and concerned with the development of individuals and of peoples. *Humanae Vitae*, for example, Pope Paul's 1968 encyclical on birth control, is not concerned with "purely individual morality [but] indicates the *strong links between life ethics and social ethics...*" (no. 15).

This brings us to Benedict's final and, in a way, surprising point: that development is a vocation. "Paul VI taught that progress, in its origin and essence, is first and foremost a *vocation*" (no. 16). In other words, if we view development as more than simply an increase in material well-being, we can see that to develop means (quoting Paul VI) to "do more, know more and have more in order to be more" (no. 18). This is similar to what St. John Paul II wrote in *Centesimus* (no. 36), when he criticized

> a style of life which is presumed to be better when it is directed toward "having" rather than "being," and which wants to have more, not in order to be more but in order to spend life in enjoyment as an end in itself.

Thus we are meant to make use of goods of both body and mind for the sake of our vocation, a vocation that, as Benedict notes, "applies to both the natural plane and the supernatural plane..." (no. 18). Ultimately, then, our vocation of development in this life connects with our vocation to eternal life in heaven. In this way Benedict XVI sets the concept of development in a rich context of man's natural and supernatural growth, which of course are intimately interrelated. He develops these themes in the chapters of the encyclical that follow.

"Human Development in Our Time" is the title of the second chapter. Benedict begins with a simple but significant sentence: "Paul VI had an *articulated vision of development*" (no. 21). Quite often people talk about things without bothering to define either what they are or what their purposes are. We simply repeat a term without stopping to think if we really know what it means. Development is a good example. Most people probably assume, without analysis, that it means simply increasing incomes and wealth, building infrastructure, and so on. But Benedict notes that while Paul VI certainly included economic betterment as part of development, he did not limit it to material ends. "Development needs above all to be true and integral. The mere fact of emerging from economic backwardness, though positive in itself, does not resolve the complex issues of human advancement..." (no. 23.) This understanding of development has been more or less explicit in all of the papal social documents, for the Church has never lost sight of the fact that man's primary locus of happiness and his final end are not on earth but in heaven, and one is therefore not surprised to see this theme repeated and emphasized again and again in papal teaching.

In chapter three of this book we saw that John XXIII, and even more Paul VI, directed their teaching to the new realities of the international economy, what we today call globalization. But Benedict points out that this trend has accelerated even more since the 1960s.

> The world that Paul VI had before him...was still far less integrated than today's world.... Production took place predominantly within national boundaries, and financial investments had somewhat limited circulation outside the country.... (no. 24)

Today, of course, this is greatly changed. When economic activity was largely confined within national boundaries, "states could still determine the priorities of the economy and to some degree govern its performance using the instruments at their disposal" (ibid.). But this is no longer necessarily the case. Thus the task and role of the state "need to be prudently reviewed and remodeled [and] one could foresee an increase in the new forms of political participation, nationally and internationally..." (ibid.). Later in this encyclical Pope Benedict will take up this question in more detail with some specific suggestions for new institutions and policies.

Another effect of globalization has been "new forms of competition between States as they seek to attract foreign businesses to set up production centers..." (no. 25). But this competition has led to "deregulation of the labor market [and] *a downsizing of social security systems*...with consequent grave danger for the rights of workers..." (ibid.). Hence the Church's traditional support for the labor movement "must therefore be honored today even more than in the past..." (ibid.). This point had been emphasized previously, especially by Leo XIII and Pius XI.

Benedict continues his reflections on various aspects or results of development and the globalizing process, for example, its effects on culture (no. 26). This includes the efforts of some "non-governmental Organizations... to spread abortion [and] sterilization in poor countries.... Moreover,... development aid is sometimes linked to specific health-care policies which *de facto* involve the imposition of strong birth-control measures" (no. 28).

Following this, Benedict XVI in the next two sections points out the necessity of having appropriate interdisciplinary knowledge and charity in our approach to development: "The demands of love do not contradict those of reason" (no. 30). Finally, in the last two sections of this chapter he sums up a number of points and gives a conditional judgment on the situation of today, noting that "the demands of justice require...that economic choices do not cause disparities in wealth to increase in an excessive and morally unacceptable manner" (no. 32), and that an emphasis on "short-term profits," including reducing "the level of protection accorded to the rights of workers, or abandoning mechanisms of wealth redistribution in order to increase the country's international competitiveness, hinders the achievement of lasting development" (32). Even after considering all this, including the fact that the development called for by Paul VI has not always taken place — "and in some cases one can even speak of a deterioration" (no. 33) — Benedict gives a cautiously favorable and qualified judgment of globalization: "In itself it represents a great opportunity. Nevertheless, without the guidance of charity in truth, this global force could cause unprecedented damage and create new divisions within the human family" (no. 33). The pontiff here continues in that tradition of realism that marked his predecessors in the social apostolate, who always took the existing situation as their starting point for whatever reforms they advocated. The popes have always addressed themselves to the actual state of the world, however good or bad that might have been at the time they wrote.

Chapter three of the encyclical is entitled, "Fraternity, Economic Development and Civil Society." In the first section (no. 34), Pope Benedict discusses one of the most important points in the whole ethical evaluation of economic activity: the effect of original sin on man's economic behavior.

> In the list of areas where the pernicious effects of sin are evident, the economy has been included for some time now.... Then, the conviction that the economy must be autonomous, that it must be shielded from "influences" of a moral character, has led man to abuse the economic process in a thoroughly destructive way. (no. 34)

The fundamental principle of free-market economics is that the economy is largely autonomous, that it works on its own, fueled solely by individuals' desires for their own gain, and that as a result it promotes the good of the whole. But this is to leave God out of it, and assumes that human actions undertaken for selfish or self-interested motives always somehow result in the good. In the presence of original sin this is a fiction, but a fiction that has a firm hold over many people's minds today. Benedict goes to the root of the matter by pointing out that this market fundamentalism ignores the actuality of human sin.

> Economic activity cannot solve all social problems through the simple application of *commercial logic*. This needs to be *directed towards the pursuit of the common good*, for which the political community in particular must also take responsibility. Therefore, it must be borne in mind that grave imbalances are produced when economic action, conceived merely as an engine for wealth creation, is detached from political action, conceived as a means for pursuing justice through redistribution. (no. 36)

As the popes in their social teaching have pointed out again and again, the market cannot be an ultimate arbiter of the economy; it must be shaped and guided, directly and indirectly, by those charged with care of the common good. This is because "*every economic decision has a moral consequence*" (no. 37). In response to this fact, Pope Benedict suggests various approaches, including "economic activity carried out...according to principles other than those of pure profit," "the logic of the unconditional gift," "commercial entities based on mutualist principles and pursuing social ends" (no. 38), and "economic forms based on solidarity" (no. 39).

Finally, in the last section of chapter three, Benedict XVI again discusses globalization. It should not be viewed "in fatalistic terms, as if the dynamics involved were the products of anonymous impersonal forces." Moreover (quoting John Paul II), "globalization, *a priori*, is neither good nor bad. It will be what people make of it." It does, when "suitably understood and directed, open up the unprecedented possibility of large-scale redistribution of wealth on a worldwide scale" (no. 42). Since the course of globalization is not beyond the control of human intelligence and will, "it will be possible to experience and to *steer the globalization of humanity in relational terms, in terms of communion and the sharing of goods*" (ibid.)

Chapter four, entitled "The Development of People — Rights and Duties — the Environment," deals with several topics related to the theme of duties, rights, and the economy. "Many people today would claim that they owe nothing to anyone, except to themselves.... Hence it is important to call for a renewed reflection on how *rights presuppose duties...*" (no. 43). The first example Pope Benedict brings up is the problem "associated with *population growth*" (no. 44). While "due attention must obviously be given to responsible procreation," he also notes "the signs of crisis observable in societies that are registering an alarming decline in their birth rate." Naturally, an ethic that reduces sexuality "merely to pleasure or entertainment" contributes to such a situation (ibid.).

Then Benedict XVI devotes several sections "to the duties arising from *our relationship to the natural environment*" (no. 48). As part of our "care and preservation of the environment," we need "to give due consideration to *the energy problem*" (no. 49). In fact, "the technologically advanced societies can and must lower their domestic energy consumption" and we need "a worldwide redistribution of energy resources" (no. 49). Pope Benedict notes, as did St. John Paul II, the connection between our treatment of the natural environment and our treatment of our fellow man. "*The way humanity treats the environment influences the way it treats itself, and vice versa*" (no. 51). Hence "If there is a lack of respect for the right to life and to a natural death... the conscience of society ends up losing the concept of human ecology and along with it, that of environmental ecology.... Our duties towards the environment are linked to our duties towards the human person..." (ibid.). Catholics above all ought to be aware of this truth proclaimed by Pope Benedict, even if the secular world insists that concern for the rights of the unborn and concern for our natural environment are somehow incompatible and opposed to each other. Those who are involved in one or the other of these pressing concerns should therefore look upon the other activity as worthy of respect and part of the Catholic apostolate appropriate to this era.

The next chapter is called "The Cooperation of the Human Family." *Family* here means the entire human race, and Benedict first turns his attention to the spiritual or social poverty that men can experience. "One of the deepest forms of poverty…is isolation" (no. 53). This isolation can arise from varying causes. Sometimes it results from rejection by others—"not being loved or…[having] difficulties in being able to love." But it can also come about "by man's basic and tragic tendency to close in on himself." But as "a spiritual being, the human creature is defined through interpersonal relations" (ibid.). This leads Pope Benedict to note that "development can be identified with the inclusion-in-relation of all individuals and peoples within the one community of the human family…" (no. 54). Indeed, "the Christian revelation of the unity of the human race presupposes a *metaphysical interpretation of the 'humanum' in which relationality is an essential element*" (no. 55).

Benedict next devotes several sections of this chapter to some reflections on the "contribution to development" (no. 56) that religion can offer. Although aware of the varying forms of religion and of their potential for cooperation, he notes that "religious freedom does not mean religious indifferentism, nor does it imply that all religions are equal" (no. 55).

One topic of great importance taken up by Benedict XVI in this chapter is that of finance. If we think about the purpose of an economy it should be obvious that finance by its nature is subordinate to the production of real goods and services. It is not an end in itself. Thus this sector of the economy "now needs to go back to being an *instrument directed towards improved wealth creation and development*. Insofar as they are instruments, the entire economy and finance…must be used in an ethical way…" (no. 65). As an example of ethical financial activity, Benedict instances "the experience of credit unions." Immediately after this, he takes up a subject that is perhaps unexpected, but is of great significance: usury. He writes:

> Furthermore, the *experience of micro-finance*, which has its roots in the thinking and activity of the civil humanists—I am thinking especially of the birth of pawnbroking—should be strengthened and fine-tuned. This is all the more necessary in these days when financial difficulties can become severe for many of the more vulnerable sectors of the population, who should be protected from the risk of usury and from despair. The weakest members of society should be helped to defend themselves against usury, just as poor peoples

should be helped to derive real benefit from micro-credit, in order to
discourage the exploitation that is possible in these two areas. (ibid.)

The reference to "the birth of pawnbroking," as the English translation of
the encyclical puts it, might seem odd, for pawnbroking is often associated
with exploitative lending practices toward the poor. But this is actually
a mistranslation and its meaning becomes clear when one looks at the
Latin text, as well as the versions in the Romance languages (all available
on the Vatican website). For instead of "the birth of pawnbroking," the
Latin text has "de Montibus Pietatis constitutis," while the French has
"la création des Monts de Piété," the Italian, "alla nascita dei Monti di
Pietà," and the Spanish, "el origin de los Montes de Piedad." Benedict
was referring here to the medieval *montes pietatis*, which were non-profit
institutions established by civil or ecclesiastical authority to lend money
at a low interest rate, sufficient to cover the costs of administration. The
Fifth Lateran Council in 1515 specifically granted approval to the *montes*
and exonerated them from the charge of usury; for unlike the usurer,
who sought to profit by virtue of the loan contract itself, without regard
to any expenses or loss that he might undergo, the *montes* sought only to
cover expenses, much as credit unions do today. It is often but wrongly
said that the Church has changed her teaching on the morality of taking
usury. This passage from *Caritas in Veritate*, as well as other authoritative
documents, makes clear that this is false, and that the Church's teaching
on usury remains what it always was.[5]

Benedict then concludes the chapter by touching on a variety of topics, including the importance of labor unions, "which have always been
encouraged and supported by the Church" (no. 64), and the need to
establish some kind of international authority

> to be vested with the effective power to ensure security for all, regard
> for justice, and respect for rights [including] the authority to ensure
> compliance with its decisions from all parties, and also with the coor-
> dinated measures adopted in various international forums. (no. 67)

One sees here in the great variety of subjects and proposals made by
Benedict XVI a continuation of the tradition begun by Leo XIII and Pius

---

5 See Appendix I for a full discussion of the question of usury.

XI, a tradition that recognized the complexity of the international economic scene and the need for institutions with the flexibility to respond
to mankind's actual needs according to the current situation.

In the final chapter, entitled "The Development of Peoples and Technology," Pope Benedict consciously returns to the theme of Paul VI's
encyclical, *Populorum Progressio*, the development of peoples. Benedict
points out that it is free persons who develop, a development that "is not
simply the result of natural mechanisms, since... we are all capable of
making free and responsible choices" (no. 68). Rather, this development
"today is closely linked to *technological progress...*" (no. 69). Although
technology, Benedict asserts, "is a profoundly human reality, linked to the
autonomy and freedom of man" (no. 69), nevertheless it "can give rise to
the idea that technology is self-sufficient" and it "can appear ambivalent"
(no. 70). For "true development does not consist primarily in 'doing,'"
and "will never be fully guaranteed through automatic or impersonal
forces..." (no. 71).

One of the most obvious examples of "technological development is the
increasingly pervasive presence of the *means of social communications*"
(no. 73). But these can serve "economic interests intent on dominating
the market" or seek "to impose cultural models that serve ideological
and political agendas" (ibid.). Just as with other kinds of technology, "the
*meaning and purpose of the media must be sought within an anthropological
perspective,*" that is, "when they are geared towards a vision of the person
and the common good that reflects truly universal values" (ibid.).

Likewise "the field of *bioethics*" is another area of technology "where
the very possibility of integral human development is radically called
into question" (no. 74). Thus the social question "concerns not just how
life is conceived but also how it is manipulated, as biotechnology places
it increasingly under man's control" (no. 75). That, along with "a pro-eu-
thanasia mindset... are cultural viewpoints that deny human dignity
[and] foster a materialistic and mechanistic understanding of human life"
(ibid.). Pope Benedict then goes to the root of these concerns, which is
"the tendency to consider the problems and emotions of the interior life
from a purely psychological point of view, even to the point of neurological
reductionism" (no. 76.) "The supremacy of technology tends to prevent
people from recognizing anything that cannot be explained in terms of
matter alone" (no. 77). But such reductionism is wrong.

The development of individuals and peoples is likewise located on a height, if we consider *the spiritual dimension* that must be present if such development is to be authentic. It requires new eyes and a new heart, capable of *rising above a materialistic vision of human events*.... By following this path, it is possible to pursue the integral human development that takes its direction from the driving force of charity in truth. (ibid.)

Benedict XVI ends his encyclical with a short conclusion. Here he stresses our immense need for God if we are to accomplish genuine development.

In the face of the enormous problems surrounding the development of peoples, which almost make us yield to discouragement, we find solace in the sayings of our Lord Jesus Christ, who teaches us: "Apart from me you can do nothing," and then encourages us: "I am with you always, to the close of the age." As we contemplate the vast amount of work to be done, we are sustained by our faith that God is present alongside those who come together in his name to work for justice. (no. 78)

But this work requires "a truly integral humanism ..., a Christian humanism.... *A humanism which excludes God is an inhuman humanism*" (ibid.).

For this reason, even in the most difficult and complex times,...we must above all else turn to God's love. Development requires...reliance upon God's providence and mercy, love and forgiveness, self-denial, acceptance of others, justice and peace. (no. 79)

With this Benedict concludes where he began, with that "charity in truth, to which Jesus Christ bore witness by his earthy life and especially by his death and resurrection..." (no. 1). And like most of his predecessors in their social encyclicals, he entrusts the task of implementing his encyclical to the Blessed Virgin, to

obtain for us, through her heavenly intercession, the strength, hope and joy necessary to continue to dedicate ourselves with generosity to the task of bringing about the "*development of the whole man and of all men*." (no. 79)

After the unexpected resignation of Benedict XVI, Pope Francis was elected to the See of Peter in March 2013. As of this writing, he has not issued any encyclicals or other documents exclusively devoted to economic morality. However, he has issued two documents, the apostolic exhortation *Evangelii Gaudium*, November 2013, and the encyclical *Laudato Si'*, May 2015, each of which, especially the latter, devotes considerable space to that subject. Although *Laudato Si'*, whose formal title is *On Care for Our Common Home*, is concerned with man's physical environment, it recognizes the intimate connection between care for the environment and man's economic activity. Insofar as these documents concern the Church's teaching on economic morality they merit discussion here.

In both these documents Pope Francis stresses one of the key points of Catholic social doctrine, the necessity that economic life, like any other human activity, submit itself to the moral law and serve the common good. To effect this, we must erect laws and public structures to orient the economy toward that end. Free competition does not magically substitute itself for either morality or external restraints. Pius XI's remarks on this in *Quadragesimo Anno*, that "the proper ordering of economic affairs cannot be left to the free play of rugged competition [which] cannot be an adequate controlling principle in economic affairs" (no. 88), and Francis's statement in *Evangelii Gaudium* that "we can no longer trust in the unseen forces and the invisible hand of the market" (no. 204), are simply two expressions of the same truth taught over and over again by the Magisterium.

Likewise on other points, Francis is simply repeating what his predecessors have said. On the question of the distribution of wealth, for example, Leo XIII noted that "there is the party which holds the power because it holds the wealth," and then "there is the needy and powerless multitude, sore and suffering…" (*Rerum Novarum*, no. 47). Thus when Pope Francis notes in *Evangelii Gaudium*, no. 56, that "the earnings of a minority are growing exponentially, [and] so too is the gap separating the majority from the prosperity enjoyed by those happy few," we can see that this kind of concrete judgment about economic conditions has ample precedent in the teachings of prior popes. Likewise, Pope Francis's rejection of "the absolute autonomy of markets and financial speculation" (*Evangelii Gaudium*, no. 202), differs not at all from St. John Paul II's demand "that the market be appropriately controlled by the forces of society and by the State…" (*Centesimus Annus*, no. 35).

Although the subject of the encyclical *Laudato Si'* is care for the earth that God has given us as our common dwelling place, any discussion dealing with the earth as our home must treat economic matters extensively, since man's economic activity necessarily affects his environment. Hence the attention to economics in this encyclical. The fundamental reason advanced by Pope Francis as to how and why economic activity carried on in the spirit of human selfishness and regulated by little or nothing except market forces harms the physical environment is precisely the same reason as that advanced by his predecessors to explain how and why economies structured in such manner harm human society. Human greed does not promote human flourishing, and there is absolutely no reason to expect such greed to somehow produce beneficent results either for society or for the physical environment. "Yet by itself the market cannot guarantee integral human development and social inclusion," writes Francis (no. 109). Surely we can see here a repetition of the many utterances made by previous popes (and quoted at length in this volume) on the insufficiency of the free market as a means to a just economic order. For just as we cannot expect that free competition will infallibly work toward the good of humanity, similarly we can hardly expect that the health of "our common home," the earth, can "be left to the free play of rugged competition," as Pius XI put it (*Quadragesimo Anno*, no. 88). Indeed, as Francis writes further: "Caring for ecosystems demands farsightedness, since no one looking for quick and easy profit is truly interested in their preservation" (*Laudato Si'*, no. 36).

Leo XIII himself had noted that "the earth, though divided among private owners, ceases not thereby to minister to the needs of all" (*Rerum Novarum*, no. 8), and this teaching has been repeated again and again by his successors. St. John Paul II noted in particular that Leo XIII was "well aware that private property is not an absolute value, nor [did] he fail to proclaim the necessary complementary principles, such as the *universal destination of the earth's goods*" (*Centesimus Annus*, no. 6). Thus Francis simply sums up the teaching of the Church when he writes:

> The Christian tradition has never recognized the right to private property as absolute or inviolable, and has stressed the social purpose of all forms of private property. (*Laudato Si'*, no. 93)

And more so than with objects of individual ownership is it the case that, the natural environment is a collective good, the patrimony of all humanity and the responsibility of everyone. If we make something our own, it is only to administer it for the good of all. (no. 95)

If it is true that mankind cannot depend upon market forces to promote economic justice or to provide adequate protection for the common environment, then it follows that economic forces must be restrained, a point that (as we have seen) the sovereign pontiffs have insisted upon again and again. Thus Francis writes: "Politics must not be subject to the economy, nor should the economy be subject to the dictates of an efficiency-driven paradigm of technocracy" (no. 189).

Once more, we need to reject a magical conception of the market, which would suggest that problems can be solved simply by an increase in the profits of companies or individuals. Is it realistic to hope that those who are obsessed with maximizing profits will stop to reflect on the environmental damage which they will leave behind for future generations? (no. 190)

The realization that a single-minded effort toward "maximizing profits" will inevitably cause harm to our environment suggests another point—namely, that "a decrease in the pace of production and consumption can at times give rise to another form of progress and development" (no. 191). Further, "we need also to think of containing growth by setting some reasonable limits and even retracing our steps before it is too late" (no. 193). Earlier John Paul II had written:

Equally worrying is the *ecological question* which accompanies the problem of consumerism and which is closely connected to it. In their desire to have and to enjoy rather than to be and to grow, people consume the resources of the earth and their own lives in an excessive and disordered way. (*Centesimus Annus*, no. 37)

In other words, when our notion of the good for mankind is chiefly the possession of more and more things, not only do we harm our physical surroundings, but we do damage to our own selves, in both body and soul. Therefore "a decrease in the pace of production and consumption can at times give rise to another form of progress and development"(*Laudato Si',* no 191), by giving us space and time in which to pay attention to the things that perfect man in body and soul. Francis notes that when such proposals are made "some react by accusing [those who suggest them] of irrationally attempting to stand in the way of progress and human development" (no. 191). But it is the critics of such proposals who are irrational, in that they see mankind's highest good as simply more and more production and consumption, regardless of whether the items produced are necessary or helpful, and regardless of whether their production inflicts seemingly irreparable harm on both the physical and the social environment.

Since God created man as an animal endowed with a rational and immortal soul, we touch on the one side the spiritual world, and on the other the material. Hence our decisions about how we live affect both ourselves and our physical surroundings. It is hardly surprising, then, that our economic life, of which industrial activity is a large part, should have a major impact on the external environment. The principles of Catholic social thought that are able to safeguard man's social and moral health are likewise able to safeguard the health of our physical environment. Of course, this should surprise no one, for it is simply an example of how the virtues of justice and charity, of solidarity and restraint, apply in one area as much as in another. As the Church of God proceeds through time on her journey to eternity, we can expect that she will apply these principles to new situations that arise or that come to her notice. The Church will always take as her model

> the Gospel image of "the scribe who has been trained for the king-dom of heaven," whom the Lord compares to a "householder who brings out of his treasure what is new and what is old" (Mt 13:52). The treasure is the great outpouring of the Church's Tradition, which contains "what is old" — received and passed on from the very begin-ning — and which enables us to interpret the "new things" in the midst of which the life of the Church and the world unfolds. (John Paul II, *Centesimus Annus*, no. 3)

SEVEN

The Authority of the
Church's Social Teaching

*Social doctrine is built on the foundation handed on by the
Apostles to the Fathers of the Church, and then received and
further explored by the great Christian doctors.*
—Benedict XVI, *Caritas in Veritate,* no. 12

T HE AUTHORITY OF CATHOLIC SOCIAL TEACHING
cannot be considered in isolation from the authority of the Church's
teaching in general. This is because Catholic social teaching is
simply part of the Church's whole complex of teaching. In fact, as St. John
Paul II pointed out, the Church's social teaching "belongs to the field...
of *theology* and particularly of moral theology" (*Sollicitudo Rei Socialis,*
no. 41). Thus before looking specifically at her social doctrine, we need
to understand the doctrinal weight of the Church's teaching as a whole.

Immediately before his Ascension, Our Lord told the apostles: "Go
therefore and make disciples of all nations,... teaching them to observe
all that I have commanded you; and lo, I am with you always, to the close
of the age" (Matthew 28:19–20). Earlier he had told them: "He who hears
you hears me, and he who rejects you rejects me, and he who rejects me
rejects him who sent me" (Luke 10:16). By these and by numerous other
statements we can understand that Jesus Christ endowed his followers,
as constituted into a hierarchical Church, with the authority to teach in
his own name. At the First Vatican Council (1870), the Church clearly
stated the obligation of Catholics to believe what is taught by the Church
in the name of Christ.

Further, all those things are to be believed with divine and Catholic
faith which are contained in the Word of God, written or handed

down, and which the Church, either by a solemn judgment or by her ordinary and universal teaching [*ordinario et universali magisterio*], proposes for belief as having been divinely revealed.[1]

We should note the Council's distinction between what is taught "by a solemn judgment or by her ordinary and universal teaching." The Church's Magisterium or teaching authority uses both these methods. The solemn or extraordinary Magisterium may be seen in definitions either by a pope or by an ecumenical (general) council, ratified by the pope. These exercises of the extraordinary Magisterium are usually accompanied by anathemas against any Catholic who would presume to dissent from such solemn teaching of the Church.

The ordinary and universal Magisterium, on the other hand, is the usual way that the Church teaches, by means of papal pronouncements, approved catechisms, or statements of bishops when these conform to papal teaching. This of course is not to say that everything that any bishop or pope has ever said is part of the ordinary and universal Magisterium. Rather, this is the normal method by which divine truths are communicated to the faithful. Moreover, we should note that the First Vatican Council refers to it as "ordinary *and* universal." "Ordinary" means that it is taught in the manner I just mentioned, and "universal" means that it is taught by all the bishops together with the supreme pontiff, and generally over a period of time.[2] Usually when a teaching has been reiterated as true and authoritative by a succession of popes and bishops, we have reason to assume that it is part of the ordinary and *universal* Magisterium, and as such must be believed as faithfully as doctrines that have been solemnly defined by a pope or council.

For the most part the moral teaching of the Church has been taught only in this manner—that is, by the ordinary and universal Magisterium. This is the case even with as important a question as abortion. There is no doubt about the fact that the Church considers abortion a grave crime; no Catholic has any legitimate reason to question the finality of Catholic moral

1 *Dogmatic Constitution on the Church*, chap. 3.

2 The Second Vatican Council in the Dogmatic Constitution on the Church (*Lumen Gentium*) no. 25, taught: "Although the bishops, taken individually, do not enjoy the privilege of infallibility, they do, however, proclaim infallibly the doctrine of Christ on the following conditions: namely, when, even though dispersed throughout the world but preserving for all that amongst themselves and with Peter's successor the bond of communion, in their authoritative teaching concerning matters of faith or morals, they are in agreement that a particular teaching is to be held definitively and absolutely."

doctrine in this area. Yet there has never been a solemn pronouncement of the extraordinary Magisterium on this subject. But the ordinary and universal teaching of the Church on abortion has been clear. Even in the *Didache*, an early Catholic writing probably dating from before AD 100, abortion is condemned, and this condemnation has continued to the present day, with the encyclicals and other writings of John Paul II being noteworthy instances of this. And though some have argued that Paul VI's encyclical *Humanae Vitae* was infallible of itself, the more common view is that while the encyclical as such was not infallible, its doctrine clearly was, since the Church has always taught that contraception is against the natural and divine law. From this we can see that Catholics must embrace the totality of Catholic doctrine and reject any minimalist approach that would ignore or slight the teachings of the ordinary and universal Magisterium.

I have spoken of the Magisterium as "ordinary *and* universal." But sometimes we have a case of simply "the ordinary Magisterium." Such instances are discussed in Pius XII's 1950 encyclical *Humani Generis*, and in the Dogmatic Constitution on the Church (*Lumen Gentium*) of the Second Vatican Council (1964). Pius XII taught:

> Nor must it be thought that what is expounded in encyclical letters does not of itself demand consent, since in writing such letters the Popes do not exercise the supreme power of their teaching authority. For these matters are taught with the ordinary teaching authority [*Magisterio enim ordinario haec docentur*], of which it is true to say: "He who hears you, hears me." (no. 20)

And *Lumen Gentium* further explained:

> This loyal submission of the will and intellect [in matters of faith and morals] must be given, in a special way, to the authentic teaching authority of the Roman Pontiff, even when he does not speak *ex cathedra*, in such wise, indeed, that his supreme teaching authority be acknowledged with respect, and sincere assent be given to decisions made by him, conformably with his manifest mind and intention, which is made known principally either by the character of the documents in question, or by the frequency with which a certain doctrine is proposed, or by the manner in which the doctrine is formulated. (no. 25)

In these cases the Magisterium can be ordinary but not universal. Nevertheless it demands a "loyal submission of the will and intellect," but a submission, we should note, "conformably with his manifest mind and intention, which is made known principally either by the character of the documents in question, or by the frequency with which a certain doctrine is proposed, or by the manner in which the doctrine is formulated." These circumstances will indicate the degree and kind of "submission of the will and intellect" due to each pronouncement or teaching. As I noted, however, when a doctrine of faith or morals has been reiterated again and again, or stated in a way that indicates the pope believes it to be a part of divine revelation (or closely connected thereto) or an authentic interpretation of natural law, then Catholics do not possess the liberty of dissenting from that teaching.[3]

This teaching authority of the Church extends to matters of both faith and morals. "The ordinary and universal Magisterium of the Pope and the bishops in communion with him teach the faithful the truth to believe, the charity to practice, the beatitude to hope for" (*Catechism of the Catholic Church*, 2034). And even more explicitly:

> To the Church belongs the right always and everywhere to announce moral principles, including those pertaining to the social order, and to make judgments on any human affairs to the extent that they are required by the fundamental rights of the human person or the salvation of souls. (*CCC* 2032)

These moral principles that pertain to the social order are moral teachings even if they touch on matters of politics or economics. Pope Pius XI clearly articulated the authority of the Church in this area in 1931, in perhaps the greatest of the social encyclicals, *Quadragesimo Anno*. He wrote:

---

3 See Pope John Paul II's apostolic letter, *Ad Tuendam Fidem* (May 28, 1998) and the Doctrinal Commentary on the Concluding Formula of the *Professio Fidei* issued by the Congregation for the Doctrine of the Faith (June 29, 1998). In addition to making clear that there is no right to dissent, both these documents discuss the different ways the Church exercises her teaching authority, such as the extraordinary Magisterium, the ordinary and universal Magisterium and "the teachings which either the Roman Pontiff or the College of Bishops enunciate when they exercise their authentic Magisterium, even if they do not intend to proclaim these teachings by a definitive act" (Apostolic Letter *Motu Proprio* of Pope John Paul II *Ad Tuendam Fidem*, Appendix A, "Profession of Faith," 27).

Moreover, of course, if a teaching on faith or morals has achieved a status requiring definitive assent, it can hardly be subject to change by anyone.

We lay down the principle long since clearly established by Leo XIII
that it is Our right and Our duty to deal authoritatively with social
and economic problems...not indeed in technical matters, for which
she has neither the equipment nor the mission, but in all those that
have a bearing on moral conduct. For the deposit of truth entrusted
to Us by God, and Our weighty office of propagating, interpreting
and urging in season and out of season the entire moral law, demand
that both social and economic questions be brought within Our
supreme jurisdiction, in so far as they refer to moral issues. (no. 41)

For, though economic activity and moral discipline are guided
each by its own principles in its own sphere, it is false that the two
orders are so distinct and alien that the former in no way depends
on the latter. (no. 42)

So although to some it might seem as if the Roman pontiffs have strayed
from their mission to teach solely on faith and morals and have entered
into the realm of politics and economics, this is not the case. Indeed, it
would be very odd if the Church, divinely guided by the Holy Spirit, had
erred in such a fundamental way that the popes themselves did not properly
understand the limits of their teaching authority—and that these limits
were correctly discerned only by adherents of various schools of secular
thought, such as supporters of Austrian economics.

We have seen that not all utterances of the Magisterium, or all ecclesiastical documents, possess the same authority. This is stated explicitly in
the *Compendium of the Social Doctrine of the Church.*

In studying this Compendium, it is good to keep in mind that the
citations of Magisterial texts are taken from documents of differing
authority. Alongside council documents and encyclicals there are
also papal addresses and documents drafted by offices of the Holy
See [so that]...the reader should be aware that different levels of
teaching authority are involved.[4]

Moreover, the fact that the social teaching of the Church deals with
things as complex as the social and economic orders makes it likely that
even within individual documents, such as encyclicals, there will occur

---

4 Pontifical Council for Justice and Peace, *Compendium of the Social Doctrine of the Church*
(Washington: United States Conference of Catholic Bishops, 2004), 3.

statements of varying authority. Thus we need to pay close attention not merely to "the character of the documents in question" but also to "the frequency with which a certain doctrine is proposed [and] the manner in which the doctrine is formulated" (*Lumen Gentium*, no. 25). It is my opinion that certain things that have been taught repeatedly in the papal social encyclicals do possess infallibility by virtue of being part of the Church's ordinary and universal Magisterium. These include the following:

1. The necessity for cooperation in economic affairs and the inadequacy of free competition as a general regulating principle for an economy;
2. The duty in commutative justice to pay a just or living wage and hence the duty in social justice to organize the economy so that this duty can be fulfilled;
3. The principle of subsidiarity;
4. The right of private property alongside the social duties of property;
5. The illicitness of usury.[5]

In addition to these doctrines, which have been stated and restated many times, the encyclicals include items of lower degrees of authority, including historical observations and even simple suggestions, as Pius XI wrote in *Quadragesimo Anno*:

> In the present state of human society, however, We deem it advisable that the wage contract should, when possible, be modified somewhat by a contract of partnership, as is already being tried in various ways with significant advantage to both wage earners and employers. (no. 65)

Obviously the words "present state of human society" and "We deem it advisable" show that this is advice, not a universal command of the moral law. Of course, the fact that Pope Pius did "deem it advisable" shows that the proposal, even if only on the level of advice, is not contrary to the moral law, but rather conformable to it, and at least in some cases, is in accord with its spirit.

---

5 Usury was condemned by several early and medieval popes and councils, and this condemnation was confirmed by one of the earliest encyclicals, *Vix Pervenit* of Pope Benedict XIV (1745). See Appendix I for a full discussion of this question.

No doubt there will always be legitimate controversy over the level of authority of certain papal statements. But we would err if we attempted to reduce that teaching to a few general principles such as "Be just," or "Help the poor." The popes go much further than that in the specifics of their teaching, and, taken as a whole, their doctrine presents a particular view of economic life, clear enough so that it rules out certain economic policies as contrary to the teaching of the Church.

There is no need to mystify Catholic social doctrine. It is part of the Church's moral teaching, and just as Catholics should look to the Church when forming their consciences about their conduct as individuals or within their families, so they should look to her when forming their consciences regarding their social or economic or political conduct. As Pius XI wrote in his first encyclical, *Ubi Arcano* of December 1922:

> Great, without question, is the number of those who profess Catholic teaching concerning social authority and the due regard for it, concerning the rights and duties of laborers on land or in industry...and finally the rights of the Creator, Redeemer, and Lord, Christ Himself, over men and nations — and yet by their spoken and written word, and the whole tenor of their lives, act as if the teaching and oft-repeated precepts of the Sovereign Pontiffs...had lost their efficacy or were completely out of date. (no. 60)
>
> *In all this we recognize a kind of moral, judicial, and social Modernism, and We condemn it as strongly as We do dogmatic Modernism.* (no. 61)

APPENDIX I

The Question of Usury

I. INTRODUCTION

ALTHOUGH HARDLY AN ISSUE TODAY FOR MOST PEOPLE, the usury question has a longer history of debate and a more abundant literature than probably any other point of Catholic social doctrine. In view of the neglect it has received since the middle of the nineteenth century, is there any reason to renew that debate now? Does it have any relevance to the economic life of modern states? We will see that it does, or rather that it could, if modern societies would decide to shape their economic conduct according to the principles of morality as taught by the Church. Thus, aside from its considerable historic interest, the question of the morality of usury should be very much a live issue for Catholics today.

In order to perceive the moral status of usury, we must first understand what it is. Although today usury commonly means charging excessive interest on loans, or perhaps only on loans intended for consumptive purposes, the classical doctrine of the Church on usury and the debates among some of her outstanding theologians were concerned with another question. For usury as it was understood for centuries meant the charging of *any* interest on a loan simply based on the loan contract — that is, without any other justifying cause except that money is being loaned. The most recent relatively complete papal discussion of usury occurred in Pope Benedict XIV's encyclical of 1745, *Vix Pervenit*. The pope stated:

> The nature of the sin called usury has its proper place and origin in a loan contract...[which] demands, by its very nature, that one return to another only as much as he has received. The sin rests on the fact that sometimes the creditor desires more than he has given..., but any gain which exceeds the amount he gave is illicit and usurious. (III, 1)

> One cannot condone the sin of usury by arguing that the gain is
> not great or excessive, but rather moderate or small; neither can it be
> condoned by arguing that the borrower is rich; nor even by arguing
> that the money borrowed is not left idle, but is spent usefully.... (III, 2)

Nonetheless, as we will see, in this same encyclical Benedict expressly allows
for the possibility that there can be legitimate titles to interest which do
not fall under the head of usury; the central question is whether interest
is ever justified merely by virtue of a loan contract. We should keep this
point in mind as we proceed.

Usury is a question that arises at the intersection of theology, philosophy, economics, and law, and has implications for each of these subjects.
Considering the weight of the Church's consistent and centuries-long
condemnation of usury, obviously there arises a theological question of
development of dogma, as well as of the validity of venerable arguments
in scholastic moral theology and moral philosophy, in canon law, and in
the teachings of economic theory. I will treat the subject mainly, however,
from the standpoint of moral philosophy and theology, which, along with
canon law, is where historically most of the debate was conducted.

II. HISTORICAL BACKGROUND
AND DEVELOPMENT

THE USURY QUESTION HAS AN UNUSUALLY LONG AND RICH HISTORY.
It is necessary to sketch this background, without which both the importance of the controversy and the weight of the intellectual arguments on
behalf of the Church's traditional position might not be clear. In addition,
a historical approach will help to show how gradually the essential features
of the condemnation of usury were worked out.[1]

The negative judgment upon usury in the early Church occurs against
a backdrop of wide condemnation by Greek and Roman writers and the
Old Testament. The list of classical pagan authors who disapproved of it

---

1 In my historical presentation I largely follow Patrick Cleary, *The Church and Usury: An
Essay on Some Historical and Theological Aspects of Money-Lending* (Palmdale, CA: Christian
Book Club of America, 1914; repr. 2000); and John T. Noonan, *The Scholastic Analysis of Usury*
(Cambridge: Harvard University, 1957). The latter work is exhaustive in its historical detail, but
the author clearly holds a bias in favor of the ultimate vacuity of the usury prohibition.

is impressive and includes Plato,[2] Aristotle,[3] Aristophanes,[4] and Seneca.[5] In addition to a general condemnation of usury by some of the best minds of the classical world, Roman law provided the legal concept from which canon law would later draw its fundamental analysis of the usury question. This was the Roman law contract of *mutuum*, and one can hardly overestimate its importance for understanding the usury question in the medieval period and thereafter.

> The subject-matter of the *mutuum* must consist of things that can be measured, weighed, or numbered, such as wine, corn, or money; that is, things which being consumed can be restored *in genere*....
> From the nature of this contract the obligation is imposed upon the borrower to restore to the lender, not the identical thing loaned, but its equivalent — that is, another thing of the same kind, quality, and value....
>
> With regard to the responsibility for loss, since from the peculiar character of the contract the right of consumption passes to the borrower, the latter is looked upon as the practical owner of the thing loaned, and he therefore holds it entirely at his own risk....[6]

The two characteristics of the *mutuum* contract that were to figure so greatly in subsequent discussions about usury were first, that the actual good loaned was not returned but rather consumed in some manner by the borrower, and second, that the borrower was considered to be the owner of the borrowed goods for all practical purposes. This is in contrast to the loan or rent of something that will be physically returned, such as a house or a car.

---

2 *Laws*, bk. V, 742.

3 *Politics*, bk. I, 10, 11. Since Aristotle's opinion on usury was the one most cited of all pagan authors during the Middle Ages, I reproduce it here: "The most hated sort [of wealth-getting], and with the greatest reason, is usury, which makes a gain out of money itself, and not from the natural object of it. For money was intended to be used in exchange, but not to increase at interest. And this term interest, which means the birth of money from money, is applied to the breeding of money because the offspring resembles the parent. Wherefore of all modes of getting wealth this is the most unnatural" (1258b, Oxford translation). Too much stress should not be put on his statement about "the breeding of money" taken in isolation, for the question of whether money can be fruitful is in large part a semantic question.

4 *Clouds*, 1283 ff.

5 *De Beneficiis*, bk. VII, 10.

6 William C. Morey, *Outlines of Roman Law*, 2nd ed. (New York: G. P. Putman's Sons, 1914), 355–56.

The Old Testament also contains numerous strictures against usury.[7] Although those in the Pentateuch limit the prohibition only to fellow Israelites, the later passages, for example Psalm 15 and Ezekiel, are phrased as if they are meant to apply universally. I think the way to regard both the pagan and Jewish usury prohibitions is to see them as part of a general framework of disapproval of usury, without stressing too much the reasons given in any particular text.[8] Usury was suspect, it had a bad odor, the upright did not exact it. This general but not absolute condemnation of usury was the inheritance of the Church and explains the fact that some of the early canons seem to condemn usury only when taken by clerics, although there are also decisive prohibitions of it as intrinsically unjust.[9]

The Church first manifests her own opposition to usury during the Patristic period. Numerous writers condemn usury, including Apollonius, Clement of Alexandria, Tertullian, Cyprian, Basil, Gregory of Nyssa, Ambrose, Augustine, Jerome, and John Chrysostom. In addition, the Apostolic Canons, dating in their final form to around 380, prohibit the taking of usury by the clergy (44th canon), as do the Council of Arles in 314 (12th canon) and the First Council of Nicaea in 325 (17th canon) — while the Council of Elvira in 305 or 306, the First Council of Carthage in 345 (12th canon) and the Council of Aix in 789 (36th canon) prohibit it to the laity also.[10]

Many of the Patristic utterances against usury are in the form of denunciations of exploitation of the poor, and thus do not state whether usury is an offense against justice or only against charity, or even whether it is simply prohibited by the positive law of the Church. But among the Patristic strictures on usury two deserve special mention. The first is the letter of Leo the Great, *Ut nobis gratulationem*, issued in October 443 and

---

7   Exodus 22:25, Leviticus 25:36–37, Deuteronomy 23:19–20, Nehemiah 5:7–10, Psalm 15:5, Proverbs 28:8, Jeremiah 15:10, Ezekiel 18:8, 13, 17, and 22:12.

8   "The modern Rabbis give an extremely interesting explanation of the Torah permission. There was, they say, at that time no law amongst the Gentiles which prohibited the practice of usury; and it was only equitable that the Jews should be entitled to exact usury of a people who might exact it of them. In this way, by a system of compensation the Jews were secured against impoverishment by the payment of usury, since what was paid in usury by some, was recovered by other members of the race." Patrick Cleary, *The Church and Usury*, 7.

9   That an atmosphere of disapproval of usury existed throughout the Jewish and Christian spheres of intellectual influence is clear also from the denunciations of usury in the Koran. See 2:275–6, 3:130, 4:161, and 30:39.

10   Arthur Vermeersch, "Usury," *The Catholic Encyclopedia* (New York: Robert Appleton, 1912), 15:235. The authenticity of the condemnation by Elvira of lay usury is doubtful.

addressed to the bishops of Campania, Picene, and Tuscany.[11] This contained a section dealing with usury, known from its opening words, *Nec hoc quoque*. John Noonan calls it "the single most important document of the early Church on usury."[12] It is important because it proceeds from the supreme ecclesiastical authority, because it clearly includes the laity in its prohibition, and because it singles out usury as intrinsically unjust — not simply as one of many uncharitable practices that exploit the poor.

The second item is a remarkable statement known as *Ejiciens*, once attributed to St. John Chrysostom, but now thought to be from the fifth century. It was later incorporated by Gratian in the Church's canon law and anticipates the classical form of the argument against usury that St. Thomas gives. It presents the clearest rationale for the usury prohibition of any of the early documents. It is worth quoting at length.

> Of all merchants, the most cursed is the usurer, for he sells a good given by God, not acquired as a merchant acquires his goods from men; and after the usury he reseeks his own good, taking both his own good and the good of the other. A merchant, however, does not reseek the good he has sold. One will object: Is not he who rents a field to receive the fruits or a house to get an income similar to him who lends his money at usury? Certainly not. First, because money is only meant to be used in purchasing. Secondly, because one having a field by farming receives fruit from it; one having a house has the use of inhabiting it. Therefore, he who rents a field or house is seen to give what is his own use and to receive money, and in a certain manner it seems as if he exchanged gain for gain. But from money which is stored up you take no use. Thirdly, a field or a house deteriorates in use. Money, however, when it is lent, is neither diminished nor deteriorated.[13]

Ejiciens makes the crucial distinction between goods that must be returned to their original owner after being used, and goods such as money that are returned only in amount and kind — the subject of a contract of *mutuum*. The first type of good normally deteriorates in use and the owner can rightly charge something for the use and, of course, also expect the original

11 Denzinger (32nd edition), 280–81.
12 Noonan, *The Scholastic Analysis of Usury*, 15.
13 As quoted in Noonan, *The Scholastic Analysis of Usury*, 38–9.

thing back. But with a good that is consumed in its use, it is hard to see how one can charge for wear and tear.[14]

The reasoning of *Ejiciens* is not altogether clear in every respect, and there are more than hints of some of the popular grounds for opposing usury that were ultimately rejected because they did not stand up to examination, such as the ideas that time could not be sold and that money was purely a measure. Nevertheless, here is an early and solid grasp of the Thomistic argument, at least in germ.

Before we proceed to the scholastic period with its rich and complex discussions of usury, we would do well to sum up where we stand. Usury is clearly condemned by the Old Testament, several notable classical pagan authors, and the early Church. But many of these sources seem to condemn usury as a sin against charity, not necessarily against justice, in the sense that it is discussed in general denunciations of acts that exploit the poor. There is usually no clear reason for saying that usury is wrong, and most of the reasons tend toward the rhetorical rather than being rational examinations of what usury is and why it is wrong. But no one could read this mass of material and come away without understanding that usury offends against Christian morals, whatever the ultimate basis of its depravity might be.

The elaborate development of theories about usury began tentatively in the early Middle Ages and lasted until around the middle of the eighteenth century. The scholastic analysis of usury by no means ended with the end of the medieval period, for the same kind of reasoning and arguments, even if sometimes with different results, were employed for several centuries afterwards. In discussing this period I will proceed as follows: After some preliminary remarks I will set forth the scholastic usury teachings that have the most force, chiefly official pronouncements by the Church and the opinions of St. Thomas Aquinas. Then I will discuss the kinds of contracts that became increasingly common as means either to avoid or evade the usury prohibition, noting in particular any official reactions to them. This will bring us to the end of the period, when scholastic reasoning could be taken for granted in the world of Catholic theology and philosophy—a period that, for our purposes, conveniently coincides roughly with Benedict XIV's encyclical, *Vix Pervenit*. We should keep in mind that throughout this period hardly any Catholic attempted to justify

---

14 In *De Malo*, q. 13, a. 4, Thomas rejects the "wear and tear" argument. But despite this, it seems to me to fit well with Thomas's understanding of the question, as we will see.

the taking of usury as such; on that there was no controversy to speak of. The controversy and the complex arguments that characterize this period concern not whether or not it was licit to take interest simply because of a contract of *mutuum*. Rather, the debate was over whether various types of contracts do or do not constitute usury, and whether and when extrinsic titles can be invoked by which one may justly receive interest on a loan without it constituting usury.

During the Carolingian period, both ecclesiastical and civil authorities had promulgated numerous decrees against usury, including excommunication for laymen guilty of usury. Scholastic analysis proper may be said to begin with St. Anselm of Canterbury, "the first medieval author to suggest the similarity of usury and robbery…one of the earliest indications that usury is to be considered a sin against justice."[15] In the high Middle Ages the discussion of usury became more focused and clear. At the same time, writers sometimes took as the basis for their reprobation of usury arguments that were subsequently disavowed or that failed to find much support in other authors: for example, the idea that usury is the selling of time, the Aristotelian doctrine that money was not fruitful or that it was purely a measure, and the idea that a loan had to be gratuitous (see Luke 6:35) and thus the lender could not hope for or receive any recompense beyond a return of the principal. But the bases that were to provide the best means of understanding the sinfulness of usury were also frequently mentioned, and in the case of St. Thomas, constituted his principal argument against it. These bases are chiefly the consumptible nature of money—the fact that in loaning money the same thing is not returned, but rather something of the same kind and value, and thus ownership in a sense passes to the borrower. The important point about the development of scholastic doctrine on usury is that almost all writers sought to ground the Church's prohibition in the natural law itself, however variously they explained it.

St. Thomas's most mature discussion of usury is in the *Summa Theologiae* II-II, q. 78.[16] I will quote extensively from the Respondeo in article 1, which contains his theory in a nutshell.

> I answer that to receive usury for money loaned [*mutuata*] is in itself unjust, because that is sold which does not exist, by which clearly an inequality is constituted which is contrary to justice. For

15 Noonan, *The Scholastic Analysis of Usury*, 17.
16 See also the *De Malo*, q. 13, a. 4.

the evidence of which it must be known that there are certain things the use of which is the consumption of those things; as we consume wine by using it for drinking or we consume wheat by using it for food. Whence in such things the use of a thing ought not to be computed separately from the thing itself; but to whomever is granted the use from that fact itself is granted [possession of] the thing; and on account of this in such things through the loan [*mutuum*] ownership is transferred. If anyone therefore wishes to sell separately the wine, and again wishes to sell the use of the wine, he would sell the same thing twice, or he would sell that which does not exist; whence clearly he would sin by injustice. And by a similar reason he commits injustice who loans [*mutuat*] wine or wheat seeking to be given two recompenses; one indeed the restitution of an equal amount of the thing, the other, on the other hand, the price of the use which is called usury.

Below I will consider this argument in more detail and attempt to show how it provides a solid intellectual justification for the proposition that in a loan of *mutuum* nothing may be asked except the principal, unless some other title to interest is also present.

In addition to numerous papal condemnations and those by local councils, it is worth mentioning the several condemnations of usury by ecumenical councils during this period, including Lateran II in 1139,[17] Lateran III in 1179, Lyons II in 1274, Vienne in 1311–12,[18] and Lateran V in 1512–17. I will mention this last again in connection with the question of the *montes pietatis*.

As I have said, in view of the repeated condemnations of usury by the Church, it was extremely rare for anyone to directly defend the practice during the scholastic period. Nonetheless, the needs of business (or the greed of men) sought ways to insure a safe and guaranteed return while avoiding the sin of usury — or at least the severe canonical penalties to which usurers were subject. One such method was the *contractus trinus* or triple contract.

---

17 Denzinger (32nd edition), 716. Canon 13 forbids Christian burial to usurers.

18 Ibid., 906. "The Council of Vienne presents a variety of difficulties. With the exception of some fragments, the acts of the Council have perished.... Joannes Andreas...tells us that Pope Clement V made very considerable modifications in the constitutions...hence it is difficult to decide what decrees were passed in the Council." Cleary, *The Church and Usury*, 74–5.

Briefly, a *contractus trinus* was a three-fold contract existing between two business partners. The first contract was a simple contract of partnership by which one partner provided the funds and the other did the trading. The second contract was a contract of insurance by which the active partner insured the principal of the inactive partner. The third contract was a similar contract of insurance by which the inactive partner was guaranteed a profit, smaller than the enterprise was likely to make, but guaranteed, whereas the profit of the partnership itself was always in some doubt due to uncertain business conditions, the possibility of loss, etc. The silent partner paid for the two contracts of insurance by forgoing the difference between the profit he might have made as an active partner and what he would receive as guaranteed profit, say, the difference between an expected 8% and a guaranteed 4%. Thus even if the enterprise miscarried, the active partner would be required to restore the principal plus a guaranteed profit to the inactive partner. Although a bull of Sixtus V in 1586 could be interpreted as condemning the *contractus trinus*, it was largely without effect. Theologians argued that it did not ground its condemnation of the triple contract in natural law, but was merely positive legislation on the part of the pope, and in addition that its apparent ambiguity left doubt as to exactly what contracts were included in its strictures. During the sixteenth century the triple contract became widely used even without definitive approval by the Church.

The other popular contract used to avoid usury was the *census* or rent-charge. The *census* was a curious sort of contract, at least to modern ears. In its original form someone would buy the right to receive the income, or even the actual produce, from some definite thing, such as a farm. Later, with the personal *census*, this was extended to be merely the right to a return from the work of a certain person. Or, a *census* could be established based upon the tax revenue of a city or even upon the income from another and prior *census*. In addition, the *census* contracts had many variations; for example, some provided that the *census* could be terminated at the call of the buyer, the seller, or of either party. Pope Martin V in 1425 approved the more conservative types of the *census*, but the more exotic and speculative kinds never received official approval, although they were defended by some theologians.

Both the *contractus trinus* and the *census* assumed many forms according to the needs or wishes of merchants. Even more remarkable, however, was the growth of the notion of implicit contracts. Merchants, and even the notaries who drew up contracts, often did not take the trouble to put them in the form required by theological authority (e.g., to specify clearly and distinctly the three parts of a *contractus trinus*), so that a contract document that was phrased ambiguously might appear on its face to be a contract of *mutuum*, with the guaranteed return simply an instance of usury.[19] This too found theological defenders who developed the theory that became generally accepted: if a contract — no matter how its wording ran — could be analyzed into some acceptable type, then it was licit. Merchants needed to have only an implicit intention of entering into some kind of licit contract, even if they could not state what that was. "Not only were the effects of the triple contract and *census* those of a loan, but even their form did not need to be explicitly different from a loan, if the form could be analytically reduced to a licit contract."[20]

Although among Catholics usury as such still found almost no defenders in the sixteenth and seventeenth centuries, theological opinion — working hand in hand with the inventiveness of merchants and lawyers — had succeeded in furnishing several substitutes that allowed for both safety of the principal and a guaranteed return. But before discussing the dramatic but confusing turn of affairs after 1745, we must look at the titles to legitimate interest on loans that had been developing since the Middle Ages. They ultimately became more significant than either the *contractus trinus* or the *census* because they could be applied to a loan contract directly and without any need to use a particular form of words in drawing up the contract. These were the titles to legitimate interest that were considered extrinsic to the *mutuum* contract itself; that is, they might or might not exist depending on extrinsic circumstances, even if some of these circumstances were nearly always present. These were chiefly *lucrum cessans* and *damnum emergens*.

Lucrum cessans and *damnum emergens* are in a sense two sides of the same coin. The first refers to the profit that someone might have made with his money had he not instead made a loan of *mutuum*, and the second is damage or loss that a lender suffered or might suffer because he did not have access to his money for the duration of a loan. Admitted in principle, at least in isolated cases, early in the debate, they became generally

19 Cleary, *The Church and Usury*, 154–55. Duke William V of Bavaria in 1581 had tried to stop this movement toward easy acceptance of loosely-worded contracts by drawing up several model contracts for use by his subjects.

20 Noonan, *The Scholastic Analysis of Usury*, 279.

accepted later. One point to note, however, is that here the question of one's intention in making a loan — a point that loomed large at certain times in the usury debates — must be mentioned. If a merchant accustomed to trading used a sum of money for a loan of *mutuum* instead of a business venture, then clearly he could claim *lucrum cessans*, since he was always engaged in profitable activities with his money. But what of someone who simply wanted a safe means of earning a return? It is true that theoretically he could engage in trade and therefore qualify for *lucrum cessans*; but in many cases there was no real likelihood that he would do so, either through inexperience or fear of loss. I raise this point here in connection with the extrinsic titles, and we will look at it again when I present the moral questions of lending in today's economy.

One last subject that must be mentioned in our historical review are the *montes pietatis*.[21] These were institutions, usually sponsored by municipal governments or the Church, that made loans at low rates of interest to provide an alternative to usurers. They were similar to pawn shops in that they required a pledge to be left to cover the possibility of the loan not being repaid. As a rule they charged interest to cover their expenses, including salaries of their employees. Was this interest usury, and therefore were the *montes* illicit despite the good intentions of their founders? Previously it had been generally held that a loan of *mutuum* could be made only by a merchant who diverted funds to a loan, and probably out of charity toward the borrower. Justifying the *montes* seemed to open the way for justifying lending itself as a business; for if the *montes* could charge for their employees' salaries, why could not a private pawnbroker do the same? Because of such considerations, they had many opponents, but the popes gave their approbation to numerous individual *montes* throughout Italy, and definitive approval came in 1515 with their acceptance by the Fifth Lateran Council, despite opposition by the famous Thomistic commentator, Cardinal Cajetan.[22] This approval of interest charges for expenses figures in our discussion below of licit and illicit interest.

Questions concerning what was and was not usury continued to be debated, sometimes bitterly, by theologians throughout Catholic Europe down to the middle of the eighteenth century. At this point (1745) there appeared the papal encyclical, *Vix Pervenit*, already mentioned. *Vix Pervenit*

---

21 On the *montes*, see Cleary, *The Church and Usury*, 106–13; Noonan, *The Scholastic Analysis of Usury*, 294–310; and Umberto Benigni, "Montes Pietatis," *The Catholic Encyclopedia*, 10:534–36.

22 For the text of the decree, see Denzinger (32nd edition), 1442–44.

was the most extended discussion of usury ever to come forth from a pope, reaffirming the essentials of the traditional teaching but at the same time giving express allowance for extrinsic titles. Although originally addressed only to the bishops of Italy, and thus not a teaching binding on the entire Church, "it was extended to the universal Church by a decree of the Holy Office of July 28, 1835."[23] Since it is the controlling authority for this discussion, I will quote it again and more fully.

> The nature of the sin called usury has its proper place and origin in a loan contract [*in contractu mutui*]. This financial contract between consenting parties demands, by its very nature, that one return to another only as much as he has received. The sin rests on the fact that sometimes the creditor desires more than he has given. Therefore he contends some gain is owed him beyond that which he loaned, but any gain which exceeds the amount he gave is illicit and usurious.
>
> One cannot condone the sin of usury by arguing that the gain is not great or excessive, but rather moderate or small; neither can it be condoned by arguing that the borrower is rich; nor even by arguing that the money borrowed is not left idle, but is spent usefully, either to increase one's fortune… or to engage in business transactions. The law governing loans consists necessarily in the equality of what is given and returned; once the equality has been established, whoever demands more than that violates the terms of the loan….
>
> By these remarks, however, We do not deny that at times together with the loan contract certain other titles — which are not at all intrinsic to the contract — may run parallel with it. From these other titles, entirely just and legitimate reasons arise to demand something over and above the amount due on the contract.[24]

Shortly after the appearance of *Vix Pervenit*, a series of events (chiefly responses from various Roman congregations) occurred that seem to some to constitute the Church's repudiation of its hitherto constant teaching. Beginning in 1822, the decisions emanated from either the Holy Office, the Sacred Penitentiary, or the Sacred Congregation of Propaganda, some of them with explicit approval by the reigning pope.[25] They were addressed

---

23 Noonan, *The Scholastic Analysis of Usury*, 357.
24 Denzinger (32nd edition), 2546–50.
25 Some of these are reproduced in Denzinger (32nd edition), 2743 and 3105–3109.

to confessors and their general tenor was the same: persons demanding interest on loans within the limits allowed by civil law should be left undisturbed and not denied absolution. Sometimes the proviso was added that penitents should be prepared to submit to any future decision of the Holy See. At the same time, Rome never retracted the doctrine of *Vix Pervenit* and even reaffirmed and applied it to the entire Church, as we saw above.[26]

After this period of acquiescence to the practice of taking interest on loans without any clear extrinsic title, we come to more recent times, when Leo XIII condemned usury in his 1891 encyclical *Rerum Novarum*.

> Rapacious usury has increased the evil [of unrestrained competition, etc.], which, more than once condemned by the Church, is nevertheless, under a different form but in the same way, practiced by avaricious and grasping men.[27]

Although Leo does not explain what he means by "under a different form," I think it is pretty clear that what he terms usury is what the Church has always meant by it, especially since he states that it has been "more than once condemned." Thus we can see this as a reaffirmation of the traditional doctrine as stated previously in *Vix Pervenit*.

Later, the 1917 Code of Canon Law (canon 1543) reads:

> If a fungible thing is given to someone in such a way that it becomes his and later is to be returned only in the same kind, no gain can be received by reason of the contract itself; but in the payment of a fungible thing, it is not in itself illicit to contract for the gain allowed by law, unless it is clear that this is excessive, or even for a greater gain, if a just and adequate title be present.[28]

Here again we see a restatement of the doctrine of *Vix Pervenit*, followed by words that seem to deny much significance to the doctrine. Then, nearly

26 Cleary, *The Church and Usury*, 169–172. In addition, in a letter to an Irish priest in 1823, Rome specifically reaffirmed the doctrine of the encyclical.

27 *Rerum Novarum*, no. 3. The Latin text reads: "Malum auxit usura vorax, quae non semel Ecclesiae judicio damnata, tamen ab hominibus avidis et quaestuosis per aliam speciem exercetur eadem."

28 The footnotes to canon 1543 refer to the decrees of Lateran V, to the encyclical *Vix Pervenit*, and to decisions of Roman congregations on usury in 1821 and 1878. Of course, the 1917 Code, since it has been abrogated by the 1983 Code, is now simply a witness to official understanding of doctrine at the time.

a hundred years later, the 2004 *Compendium of the Social Doctrine of the Church* twice condemns usury (nos. 323 and 341), though without defining it. Finally in the recent encyclical of Benedict XVI, *Caritas in Veritate* (2009), in section 65, the pope, after noting the necessity of reorienting the financial sector toward the common good, twice mentions protecting and helping to defend "the more vulnerable" or the "weakest members of society" from usury.[29] But let us now conclude our historical overview and enter into a discussion of whether and how the usury doctrine still binds consciences today.

III. WAS THERE A CHANGE
IN THE CHURCH'S TEACHING?

WITHOUT QUESTION THE VAST MAJORITY OF THOSE WHO ARE AT all aware of the usury question would say that there was at least some change or evolution in the Church's teaching, however they might want to explain it. For certainly it appears that usury is no longer a sin that Christians need worry about. But there is something curious about saying the Church's teaching has changed. When did this occur? When did usury in the sense we mean by it here cease to be a sin? If we look in the first half of the nineteenth century as the best place to locate such a change, we find no statement by the Church during that time that says anything about repudiating the teaching of *Vix Pervenit*. Rather we see the contrary. Then, in *Rerum Novarum*, Leo XIII gives a matter-of-fact reminder of the evil of usury. The 1917 Code made a straightforward assertion of the medieval doctrine in its full rigor, followed, it is true, by qualifications whose meaning and significance we will examine below. Most recently, there have been denunciations of usury in the *Compendium* and in *Caritas in Veritate*. Even John Noonan, in an article written expressly for the purpose of proving that there had been changes (or developments as he called them) in moral doctrine, admits: "Formally it can be argued that the old usury rule, narrowly construed, still stands: namely, that no

---

29 Benedict also does not say what he means by the term "usury." But there is reason to think that he had in mind the historical rather than the modern notion. In the same section of the encyclical, the English version, when speaking of "the *experience of micro-finance*," goes on to mention "the birth of pawnbroking." This might seem a strange thing to bring up until one looks at the Latin text of the encyclical, which has "de Montibus Pietatis constitutis." Clearly Pope Benedict was thinking of medieval conditions and institutions in this section.

profit on a loan may be taken without a just title to that profit."[30] It is true that he continues and says that "in terms of emphasis, of perspective, of practice, the old usury rule has disappeared." What this means and what, if anything, can or should be done about this I will take up subsequently. But I do not think that there is any special difficulty in saying that Pope Benedict XIV's teaching from 1745 still retains its force today. One can certainly find a nearly universal *de facto* neglect of the question of usury, but one looks in vain to find that the Church ever retracted, abrogated, or substantially altered her teaching on usury. Something of course did occur (and that we will try to understand and explain), but no one should have any hesitation about proclaiming the doctrine of *Vix Pervenit* as the doctrine of the Catholic Church.

We have seen that beginning in the sixteenth century interest began to be routinely justified on loans by one or more of the extrinsic titles and that about the same time the *contractus trinus* and the *census* allowed a lender nearly the same security that he might seek in a simple loan at interest. Moreover, by the late sixteenth century these contracts did not even have to be correctly drawn up in order to avoid the stigma of usury, for an implicit good intention was widely accepted as sufficient. There is no doubt that theologians, well before the nineteenth century, while formally upholding the condemnation of usury, allowed much that their medieval predecessors would have looked askance at.[31] Although some of these developments were sanctioned by Rome, by no means were all of them. The real change — not in doctrine, but in the application of that doctrine to economic life — came in the sixteenth to eighteenth centuries, not in the 1820s or 1830s. Let us try to understand what took place.

When one reads the subtle analyses of usury by the theologians of the Baroque era, one cannot help but be impressed by their painstaking efforts. Nevertheless, the increasing complexity of commercial life made it difficult to say with any assurance what was and what was not usury. Even in the fifteenth century, Pandolfo Rucellai, who had been a banker before entering the Dominican order and wrote a treatise on the morality of exchange banking, was unable to give a definite opinion on certain

---

30 John Noonan, "Development in Moral Doctrine," *Theological Studies*, 54, no. 4 (December 1993): 663.

31 Aquinas, for example, had denied *lucrum cessans* because of the merely speculative quality of the lost gain. *Summa Theologiae*, II-II q. 78, a. 2, ad 1.

points.[32] And things did not improve as time went on and as contracts
and commercial practices grew more exotic. By the beginning of the nineteenth century (or so it appears to me) the Roman authorities basically
threw up their hands and decided it was better to allow penitents to take
moderate rates of interest on loans than to continue to analyze contracts
and reach decisions on matters more and more opaque—especially since
in many or most cases some kind of just title to interest did probably exist.
In general, moralists and moral theology textbooks began to retreat from
an engagement with the facts of economic life. Fr. John Cronin notes this
as follows:

> Our moral theology texts were, in general, hopelessly out of date in
> applying moral principles to economic life. Apparently few moral-
> ists knew enough about economic facts to work out a realistic and
> complete solution. Hence moral teaching generally confined itself to
> obvious justice and injustice and clearly defined motives.[33]

In other words, when the usurious nature of a transaction was in doubt,
it was easier to say to those involved that they need not be disturbed than
it was to try to apply the principles of the usury doctrine to the complex
facts of the situation. Even more difficult was it to make the gigantic
efforts required to orient the economy away from financial speculation
and individual enrichment toward an economy based on production that
recognized the claims of society as a whole.

This change in the Church's approach to usury did not pass unnoticed.
Various authors explained it in various ways, commonly arguing that in
modern times the nature of economic activity or the function of money
differed essentially from what obtained in the Middle Ages.[34] In the last

---

32 Noonan, *The Scholastic Analysis of Usury*, 317.

33 John F. Cronin, *Catholic Social Principles: The Social Teaching of the Catholic Church
Applied to American Economic Life* (Milwaukee: Bruce, 1950), 44–45. Apparently this was nothing
new, though, since Domingo de Soto (d. 1560) complained that few theologians of his day understood the details of the banking system. Cited in Noonan, *The Scholastic Analysis of Usury*, 336.

34 Francis X. Funk in the middle of the nineteenth century suggested such an explanation
based on the changed use of money. See Noonan, *The Scholastic Analysis of Usury*, 385–87.
Heinrich Pesch proposed that the "expansion of production and commerce" and the fact that
"everyone who has the necessary funds at his disposal could actively participate in commercial
life" justified routine interest taking. *Lehrbuch der Nationalökonomie/Teaching Guide to Economics*,
trans. Rupert J. Ederer, vol. 5, book 2 (Lewiston, NY: Edwin Mellen, 2003), 197–99. John A. Ryan
stated: "The money in a loan [today] is economically equivalent to, convertible into, concrete
capital." *Distributive Justice*, 3rd ed. (New York: Macmillan, 1942), 124.

section, I will explore what really happened as we try to understand what the Church's teaching on usury should mean for Christians today.

IV. ARGUMENTATION IN SUPPORT
OF SCHOLASTIC DOCTRINE

BEFORE PROCEEDING TO LOOK AT THE SIGNIFICANCE OF THE Church's prohibition of usury for us today, I want to argue anew for the correctness of the teaching of *Vix Pervenit*, based on St. Thomas's argument that looks to the consumptible nature of money as the key point. I do this so that we might approach the usury question with a positive appraisal of the scholastic doctrine and regard it as something that must be understood rather than disregarded as a relic of the past.

We might remember that as far back as *Ejiciens*, thinkers had distinguished between something loaned which "deteriorates in use" and something which, "when it is lent, is neither diminished nor deteriorated."[35] Money is certainly the most common representative of the latter class, but not the only. As we saw, St. Thomas based his argument on the more general class of consumptible things, and I think if we look at more humble consumptibles, such as food or drink, we might be able to look at the question afresh and understand the Church's doctrine better. Let us consider the following analogy.

Suppose we have a small businessman who owns a catering service. And suppose further that all the supplies that accompany the food and drink are disposable (plastic forks, paper napkins, etc.) so that everything he provides to his customers he cannot reuse. Now what may he licitly charge his customers for? For the replacement cost of the food, drink, and disposable supplies, certainly. In addition, he may charge each customer for a share of the overhead to run his shop: for rent and utilities, for his delivery van, for any employee wages, for any legitimate interest payments he must make, and for a "return for his labor of organization and direction, and for the risk that he underwent."[36] But as regards the food and other consumptibles that he provides, it is hard to see how he can charge a customer for more than the amount purchased. If he furnishes 100 bottles

---

35 I noted above that St. Thomas rejected the "wear and tear" argument, but despite that this argument seems to me the best reason why it is licit to charge for the use of something such as a house, whose ownership is separable from its use.

36 Ryan, *Distributive Justice*, 176.

of wine, the caterer may charge what it will cost him to replace a similar kind and amount of wine. Anything that he charges a customer in addition must come from one of the other titles I mentioned above — costs incident to the running of his business and wages for his employees and himself.

This last is what is generally called *profit*, a term that is often used loosely and inexactly. As we see, Ryan reduces it to the proprietor's labor, plus his entrepreneurial abilities and risks. It is not an open-ended invitation to charge as much as the market will bear, but rather there must exist some title of justification such as Ryan enumerates. Looked at in this way, limiting reimbursement to the consumptibles sold seems obvious. Of course the caterer cannot charge for 110 bottles of wine if he delivers only 100. His profit, in reality his salary and compensation for risk, etc., comes otherwise and is not gained at the expense of expecting more in return than what he supplied.

The application of this to loans of *mutuum* can easily be seen. Someone in the business of making loans could justly take similar expenses from customers. The *montes pietatis* acted in similar fashion. Of course, the *montes* were not profit-making in the sense that they intended to earn more than their expenses, including salaries. But according to Msgr. Ryan's analysis of business, no business is profit-making in the sense that it can justly seek as wide profits as it can obtain. The owner can seek a fair "return for his labor of organization and direction, and for the risk that he underwent." Although one cannot calculate such returns with mathematical exactness, neither can one maintain that they have no theoretical limit.[37] Even if one did argue that there should be no limit on such a return for labor, skill, and risk, that is not the same as saying that usury for the lending activity itself may be taken, for we have seen that the entrepreneur can require only the same amount as the consumptible good that he has provided — "the equality of what is given and returned," as Benedict XIV taught.

In the case of our caterer, he receives immediate or nearly immediate payment for his expenditure on food and other consumptibles. A loan, however, is generally paid back after a period of time, or gradually during

---

37 "The great majority of business men in competitive industries do not receive incomes in excess of their reasonable needs. Their profits do not notably exceed the salaries that they could command as hired managers, and generally are not more than sufficient to reimburse them for the cost of education and business training, and to enable them to live in reasonable conformity with the standard of living to which they have become accustomed." Ryan, *Distributive Justice*, 190.

such a period. Is not the lender entitled to some compensation on account of this delay? No, for "the mere time differential by itself does not cause a difference in value. There must be added the possibility of earning a profit in the intervening time period."[38] In other words, one must have a title such as *lucrum cessans* or *damnum emergens* to justify receiving interest, for the mere fact of delay by itself does not equate to the right to contract for more than the principal.[39]

I have argued both that the Church has not changed her teaching on usury and that one can make a reasonable argument for the validity of the intrinsic injustice of usury. On both points, it seems to me, assent to the scholastic teaching is not where the real difficulty is. That lies elsewhere, in the question: what does it mean? Or better, does it have any meaning except as an empty and antiquated formalism? Assuming that we accept at least some of the extrinsic titles and other practices that grew up during the Renaissance, would adherence to the usury prohibition today make any real difference in our economic and legal practices?

V. APPLICATION OF USURY THEORY
TO CONTEMPORARY ECONOMIES

IF WHAT I HAVE SAID IS CORRECT, IF IT IS THE CASE THAT THE "law governing loans consists necessarily in the equality of what is given and returned" (based both on arguments from reason as well as on a failure to find that the Church ever retracted her papal and conciliar teaching on usury), then there are two chief questions that concern us in this last section. First, we have to ask what effect the intrinsic evil of usury should have on the moral conduct of the Christian. Is there anything that Christians should do or avoid in their financial or economic behavior as a result of the sinfulness of usury? Second, what meaning does usury have in an economy hopelessly enmeshed in all kinds of interest-bearing transactions as a matter of course and without a thought as to any justifying title? Given that for centuries theologians have found it easy to justify most forms of

---

38 Pesch, *Lehrbuch der Nationalökonomie/Teaching Guide to Economics*, vol. 5, book 2, 200.

39 Another way of looking at this example that yields the same conclusion is to regard a *mutuum* of money as a *sale*, as in the case of the caterer who provides 100 bottles of wine and receives as part of his total payment the price of the 100 bottles, no more and no less. If we look at money loaned as a sale of money, we see that the price of $100 is obviously $100. Any other just charges come from the same titles the caterer had: overhead expenses, wages, etc. For the product provided (money), one can charge only what it is worth, which is always its face value.

interest, are we committing the Church to a ridiculous anachronism, a relic of the past? Are we hankering after a silly formalism in order to justify something that is easier and more honest simply to call interest on a loan?

In regard to the first question, in light of the various Roman decisions of the nineteenth century and the 1917 Code, no one can be condemned for taking the legal or customary rate of interest on a loan, provided that it is not excessive. The reason for this, I argued, is that the complexity of modern finance renders it safer simply to allow moderate interest than to engage in probably fruitless endeavors to determine the presence or absence of extrinsic titles. The Church is presuming these titles to exist generally, and moreover, is making the judgment that even if in some cases they do not, it is better for the sake of consciences to ignore that fact. The remedy always exists for restitution to be made via almsgiving in case a penitent is troubled or there seems a well-founded and probable case of real usury.

Of course, it should go without saying, the interest rates of loan sharks on so-called payday or similar loans, which can reach 500% per annum, clearly have no justification for any extrinsic title and no Catholic can lawfully have anything to do with such loans.[40] Such usury is a serious offense against justice and ought to be strictly prohibited by the civil law. Unfortunately since 1978 in the United States, judicial decisions and the gradual repeal of state laws regulating usury have allowed such gross injustices to flourish.[41]

The ecclesiastical decisions of the 1820s and 1830s were addressed to confessors and did not purport to change the usury doctrine as expressed in *Vix Pervenit*. So even though no one can be criticized for taking moderate interest, I think that in some cases one can detect the presence of usury in modern interest. For example, while it is certainly correct to point out that today there is usually opportunity for productive investment (and therefore those who put money out at *mutuum* that could otherwise be invested are entitled to claim *lucrum cessans*), this reasoning does not always hold. During times of depression or recession, "the profit expectations of businessmen are likely to be so low that they would not employ

---

40 "Even higher rates of interest are not unheard of, as one Indiana payday lender offered a loan of $100 with interest of $20 per day—an APR of 7,300%." John Skees, "The Resurrection of Historic Usury Principles for Consumption Loans in a Federal Banking System," *Catholic University Law Review* 55, no. 4 (Summer 2006): 1132.

As late as the mid-1970s most state usury laws set a limit of 10%, and the model Uniform Consumer Credit Code proposed a maximum of 18%. Lawrence P. Galie, "Indexing the Principal: The Usury Laws Hang Tough," *University of Pittsburgh Law Review* 37, no. 4 (Summer 1976): 764.

41 The 1978 Supreme Court decision, Marquette National Bank v. First of Omaha Service Corp., 439 U.S. 299, made inevitable the eventual demise of state laws regulating interest rates.

men and machines on new investment projects even if you let them borrow temporarily at a zero interest rate."[42] In such cases "some savings will follow the sterile path of debt-financed consumption, with eventual repayment at the expense of current consumption."[43] In other words, in such situations a lack of consumer demand makes spending on productive investment unprofitable, so it is likely that someone putting money out at *mutuum* is not truly forgoing investment profit, because no profit is to be had for the time being. Thus when there is excess savings with no outlet for profitable use, it is hardly in accord with the common good to reward those who choose to loan by giving them a rate of interest based on a merely hypothetical opportunity cost.

We must remember that since the extrinsic titles were never given official approval except as compensation for lost opportunities for investment earnings "they can never be advanced as a justification of a general loan system based on motives of profit."[44] Thus it seems hard to justify *lucrum cessans* for those who have no real intention of making investments, simply because such opportunities are readily available to all. What of ordinary savers who desire to put their money into insured savings accounts at banks and who, because of inexperience or fear of loss, have no desire to invest in business ventures, even to buy shares of stock or mutual funds? They are not undergoing a real loss of investment income on account of their loan of money to the bank, since otherwise they might have simply hidden the money in a mattress. I do not see how the merely theoretical possibility that they could make gains from investments applies to them, since they are too risk averse to do so. Can they licitly claim interest on bank accounts and, if so, under what title? I think there is a reason for thinking such interest just, but it is not one of the extrinsic titles that theologians have approved. It is the mere fact of inflation. "He who receives a loan of money...is not held to pay back more than he received by the loan."[45] But with our ability to monitor the level of inflation in an economy, we realize that money simply left alone, as in a mattress, will actually diminish in value. Therefore payment for inflation for money deposited in a bank or credit union seems just.

---

42 Paul Samuelson, *Economics*, 9th ed. (New York: McGraw-Hill, 1973), 336.

43 John F. Cronin, *Economics and Society* (New York: American Book Co., 1939), 131.

44 John P. Kelly, *Aquinas and Modern Practices of Interest Taking* (Brisbane: Aquinas Press, 1945), 33.

45 Thomas Aquinas, *Summa Theologiae*, II-II q. 78, a. 2, ad 2.

Moreover, it does seem possible to roughly distinguish a just rate of interest, anything above which would be usury. If we consider the rate of interest on government bonds, historically the safest investment possible, as risk free for all practical purposes, we can then examine other interest rates in their light. The following discussion refers to Australian interest rates:

> For example, on 5 January 2002, the ten year government bond rate was 5.21%, and home mortgages were 6.3% while inflation was about 2.5%. The gap between home mortgage rates and government bonds of about 1.1% was due to the riskiness of lending to home buyers compared to the government. By subtracting inflation, the government bond rate is reduced to about 2.7% which is known as the real rate of interest. Markets anticipate a fall in rates, so there is a negligible liquidity preference effect. This means that 2.7% of the loan interest on government bonds, home mortgages and all other lending is purely the result of the expectation of the lender for a return in excess of the principle. That looks suspiciously like usury.[46]

This analysis justifies the interest paid on government bonds only on the basis of inflation, apparently without considering the presence or absence of any extrinsic title. Nevertheless it suggests an interesting way of approaching the question. Another method of analysis is to recall that interest legitimately taken is compensation for an investment opportunity forgone. Thus a just rate of interest could in principle be formulated based on the expected return of an investment that the lender had the opportunity of profiting by, assuming it was possible to specify a general rate of profit for any particular place and time.

> Abstracting from statutory regulation of interest, and from any special expense or risk of loss incurred by a lender...the criterion [of a just rate of interest] is the just rate of profit from investment. This does not mean that the just rate of interest is exactly the same as the just rate of profit...[for] the profits of any business are due, at least in part, to the activities of those who are running it; and also that ordinary investment involves financial risks which are not inherent in loans of money. Consequently...the just rate of interest will be

46 Garrick Small, "Rapacious Usury: Fact or Fiction?" (paper, Campion Fellowship meeting, Toongabbie, Australia, January 2002), 7. Used with permission of the author.

lower than the just rate of profit. How much lower? Evidently by as
much as corresponds to the differential advantage of lending rather
than investing.[47]

We must remember that "the modern world…has ordered its economic
affairs with little reference to moral scruples, and in such a world it is
exceedingly difficult to assess the moral implications of loan contracts."[48]
Often we will agree with T. S. Eliot's confession: "I seem to be a petty usurer
in a world manipulated largely by big usurers."[49] The point is that even
in an economy that gives and receives interest as a matter of course, we
can perhaps at times distinguish what might be legitimate interest from
what is probably usury. Although the praxis of the Church for the past
two hundred years has been not to disturb consciences on the subject, that
does not mean there is anything wrong with discussing the matter and
attempting to identify usury where it is present. An increased consciousness of the evil and the ubiquity of usury today (see *Rerum Novarum*)
cannot but help to make Christians more aware of what to our ancestors
was one of the greatest of sins.

Another benefit of discussing the presence of usury in today's financial
transactions is that it might lead to steps to establish institutions that avoid
or minimize usury. One means of overcoming loansharking, for example,
is an institution with some resemblance to the medieval *montes pietatis*,
the credit union.[50] A commercial bank has stockholders who expect to
receive a return on their investment. If establishing a commercial bank
can be considered a legitimate investment activity, then some return
for the bank stockholders is just. But still, whatever the stockholders
receive must be paid for by higher interest rates on loans and higher bank
fees. This is not the case with credit unions, which are not profit-making
institutions in that sense. Of course they pay wages to their employees,
as did the *montes pietatis*. But credit unions are simply charging for the
necessary expenses of providing loans. Since they are owned by their
members, who are both depositors and borrowers, whatever a credit
union receives beyond its expenses is returned to its members. So even

47 Lewis Watt, "Usury in Catholic Theology," in *Readings in Economics*, ed. Richard Mulcahy
(Westminster, MD: Newman, 1959), 278.

48 Kelly, *Aquinas and Modern Practices of Interest Taking*, 20.

49 *The Idea of a Christian Society* in *Christianity and Culture* (San Diego: Harcourt Brace
Jovanovich, 1939; repr. 1977), 77.

50 Pope Benedict also commends credit unions in his encyclical *Caritas in Veritate*, no. 65.

if for-profit commercial banks are a legitimate form of investment, they seem entirely unnecessary when we have the alternative of a credit union. Thus Christians should favor and work for the spread of credit unions as an alternative to the higher interest rates of commercial banks, even if those rates are free from usury.[51]

Today the only financial institutions that operate with the goal of avoiding usury altogether are Islamic banks.[52] If usury is unjust, why are not Christians as active in promoting these sorts of financial institutions as Moslems?

Let us in conclusion look briefly at a few more financial practices and institutions that Christians might promote were we to recover the zeal for economic justice that characterized Catholics at an earlier period.

> The whole Christian doctrine of property with its responsibilities of ownership which the modern world has forgotten is wrapped up in this question of money and the taking of interest thereon. If I am in possession of money, I am in possession of something that is vital to the society in which I live. I, as a Christian, therefore, have very definite responsibilities with respect to the ownership of that money. Christian morality knows of no theory of an unqualified and unconditional ownership of property of any description. Property must be used according to its true end and purpose and in the case of money that true end and purpose is as a means of exchange. Therefore, the wrongful withholding of that money from circulation for the purpose of making a profit by waiting is a misuse of property.[53]

Such a doctrine of money is akin to Paul VI's doctrine of property in *Populorum Progressio*.

---

51 One very important topic that space prevents me from taking up is the question of bank-created money. Although it would be possible for a banking system to work otherwise, ours operates by creating money as debt. Most of the money supply today originates in this way. The banking system creates money out of nothing and yet banks charge interest on this money as they loan it out to borrowers. Almost all of the interest on such loans seems to be nothing but usury. See Rupert J. Ederer, "Is Usury Still a Problem?," *Homiletic & Pastoral Review*, 84, nos. 11–12 (August–September 1984): 18–20.

52 Islamic banks claim to engage in risk-sharing agreements with their borrowers, although there is some dispute about whether in fact they do as much as they claim. See Timur Kuran, "Islamic Economics and the Islamic Subeconomy," *Journal of Economic Perspectives*, 9, no. 4, (Fall 1995): 155–173.

53 Kelly, *Aquinas and Modern Practices of Interest Taking*, 46–47.

> Private property does not constitute for anyone an absolute and
> unconditioned right. No one is justified in keeping for his exclusive
> use what he does not need, when others lack necessities…. If cer-
> tain landed estates impede the general prosperity because they are
> extensive, unused or poorly used, or because they bring hardship to
> peoples or are detrimental to the interests of the country, the common
> good sometimes demands their expropriation. (nos. 23–24)

Clearly expropriation of funds that are being used merely in idle usury
should be a last resort, and normally the law will use financial incentives
and penalties to direct such funds toward uses more in accord with the
common good. But no Catholic need be afraid to acknowledge that "the
public authority, in view of the common good, may specify more accurately
what is licit and what is illicit for property owners in the use of their possessions."[54] A Christian society, then, by outlawing true usury completely,
and by forbidding or discouraging the kinds of contracts that during the
Renaissance helped undermine the usury prohibition among both theologians and merchants, would seek to direct money toward its proper
use. Some form of credit union would be adequate to provide financing
for non-productive consumer loans. The demand for commercial credit
could be satisfied either by merchants diverting funds from investments,
and licitly claiming *lucrum cessans*, or by some form of commercial credit
union run by associations of businesses.

Just as in the Great Depression of the 1930s, so also now events are
forcing theologians and moralists to turn their attention to the economy.
But in reality, Catholics should have as lively a sense of the demands of the
moral law relative to the economy as they do relative to sexuality or war.

> In the Middle Ages, it was taken for granted God's law applied to
> the totality of life. The idea of a double standard of morality, with a
> strict code for private life and a minimum of moral obligation for
> business and public life, is an innovation based on philosophical and
> religious individualism of the eighteenth century.[55]

However far we are today from a Christian society or a Christian economy, the goal "to impress the divine law on the affairs of the earthly city"

54 Pius XI, *Quadragesimo Anno*, no. 49.
55 Cronin, *Catholic Social Principles*, 43.

(*Gaudium et Spes*, no. 43) is always present. With respect to usury the Church has been clear in setting forth a principle, a principle that must be intelligently applied to the complex circumstances of financial life, but which nonetheless is a standard for both individual and social conduct. The doctrine on usury establishes a social goal and even if we cannot give effect to that now there are various intermediate goals that we can work toward implementing. And as with all our efforts in this life, this is part of making the world a more perfect offering to the Sacred Heart of Jesus who will one day renew all things in himself.

APPENDIX II

What Does
Centesimus Annus
Really Teach?

THE TITLE OF THIS ARTICLE, "WHAT DOES *CENTESIMUS Annus* Really Teach?," seems to imply that there might be some dispute about the teaching of *Centesimus Annus*, the last of the three social encyclicals written by Pope John Paul II. And this is correct. For when *Centesimus* was issued in 1991, it generated an unusual amount of discussion. In fact, certain commentators called it a radical departure in the hundred-year-old tradition of modern Catholic social teaching, the tradition that, at least as regards economics, began in 1891 with Pope Leo XIII's encyclical *Rerum Novarum*. To see what I mean, let us take a look at what a few of these commentators said.

Peter L. Berger wrote:

> For the first time in the modern history of Catholic social doctrine, there is here an emphatic and elaborated approval of the market economy as the optimal economic arrangement in today's world.[1]

And Kenneth Craycraft opined:

> For the first time ever, a pope has explicitly endorsed the free market as the "victorious social system" in the world, and as the type of economy that ought to be proposed in all places, especially the Third World.[2]

While Michael Novak stated:

---

1 "No 'Third Way,'" in *A New Worldly Order: John Paul II and Human Freedom*, ed. George Weigel (Washington: Ethics and Public Policy Center, 1992), 62.
2 "'Having' and 'Being': John Paul II as Pastor," in ibid., 71.

> Thus Pope John Paul II has brought economic liberty...into Catholic social teaching....[3]

And finally, Fr. Robert Sirico:

> *Centesimus Annus* represents the beginnings of a shift away from the static zero-sum economic world view that led the Church to be suspicious of capitalism and to argue for wealth redistribution as the only moral response to poverty.[4]

Clearly these authors see *Centesimus* as a sort of sea-change in Catholic social teaching. But leaving aside the question of whether the Catholic notion of development of doctrine would even allow for such a drastic change in teaching, I do not think that the text of *Centesimus Annus* supports these blanket statements. I am going to argue two things here: 1) the interpretation of *Centesimus* is particularly difficult, and 2) the teaching, taken as a whole, is in line with the doctrine of Leo XIII, Pius XI, Pius XII, Paul VI, and the other popes of whom Catholic proponents of a free market are not usually too fond.

Let me begin with my first assertion: *Centesimus* is difficult to understand. I would argue that this is so for two reasons: First, *Centesimus* sometimes seems to be at variance with itself. One writer asks if *Centesimus* is "an encyclical in conflict with itself" and another characterizes it as "schizoid."[5] It is not hard to find passages in *Centesimus* that seem to contradict each other or that at least stress opposite sides of a question.[6]

---

3 "Tested by Our Own Ideals," in ibid., 139.

4 "Away From the Zero-Sum View," in ibid., 156.

5 Both from ibid., 107 and 120. The latter writer, Kenneth Minogue, states: "One critic has described the encyclical as 'schizoid,' and different passages certainly seem to advance opposing doctrines."

6 See also Tracey Rowland's comments in her book, *Culture and the Thomist Tradition After Vatican II* (London: Routledge, 2003), 44. "Daniel Finn has observed that it is frequently difficult to determine precisely where John Paul II stands, since his style of engagement with controversial questions is to make strong affirmations about goods on both sides of an argument, as well as denunciations about the dangers attendant on each. Finn calls this the habit of using 'antithetical affirmations' and suggests that its merit is that it leaves the issues open for further debate while suggesting areas which require further consideration. However, Marciano Vidal has also observed that the negative aspect of [John Paul's] approach is that it 'renders ordinary interpretative procedures problematic' and 'leaves sharp tensions unresolved'.... [This approach] also renders such statements vulnerable to being selectively quoted for a polemical purpose."

I note, moreover, that John Paul did not employ such a tactic in his first two social encyclicals, *Laborem Exercens* and *Sollicitudo Rei Socialis*.

But whatever the reason was for his employment of such a method, since John Paul is no fool, we must assume that he knew what he was doing when he put those passages in. Therefore, it seems to me, we must seek to understand the teaching of *Centesimus Annus* on a more fundamental or general level. I believe this can be done.

The second reason I think *Centesimus* is difficult to interpret is because, unlike most encyclicals, John Paul has explicitly stated that not everything in it is to be considered as the teaching of the Church's Magisterium. In no. 3 we read:

> The present encyclical seeks to show the fruitfulness of the principles enunciated by Leo XIII, which belong to the Church's doctrinal patrimony and, as such, involve the exercise of her teaching authority. But pastoral solicitude also prompts me to propose *an analysis of some events of recent history*.... However, such an analysis is not meant to pass definitive judgments, since this does not fall *per se* within the Magisterium's specific domain.

Unfortunately, the Holy Father never says which passages of the encyclical fall within the latter category, that is, which are part of the "*analysis of some events of recent history*" and thus not part of the teaching of the Magisterium. But I do not think that this is fatal to our efforts to understand *Centesimus*, as long as we employ a broad-brush approach to its interpretation. So, for both reasons, it would be a mistake to press any one passage too far, especially a passage taken out of context or a passage that seems to be in disagreement with prior papal teaching. We must try to understand the encyclical's teaching as a whole.

My second assertion is that the teaching of this encyclical is in line with prior papal teaching on the social order. And indeed, it is easy to find parallels to most of the contents of *Centesimus* in earlier papal teaching, often with a different emphasis but with much the same meaning. But instead of showing how most of the allegedly revolutionary teachings of *Centesimus* are in fact quite in agreement with the earlier doctrine, I want to proceed in a different way and concentrate on what appears to me the heart of the matter, what we might call the *logic* or essence of Catholic social teaching. This is a logic that is fully confirmed by *Centesimus*, and which squarely contradicts the logic of the free market.

The quotations I gave indicate the widespread belief that John Paul has an attitude toward a free market economic system different from that of his predecessors. In itself, of course, this ought to set us wondering, for if John Paul can change what previous popes taught about such an important matter, then what is to prevent popes in the future from changing what John Paul teaches? The important point is to look at what I call the *logic* of the free market and compare it to the *logic* of Catholic social doctrine, including the doctrine of *Centesimus Annus*. One could state the logic of the free market like this: The basic and most important economic factors in a society, factors such as prices, wages, rates of interest, exchange rates, etc., should be set simply by the give and take of market forces, chiefly the force of supply and demand, with ideally no interference by the government or any other body. If it is necessary that occasionally government should intervene in these exchanges, this should be as little and for as short a time as possible. Organizations such as labor unions, in this view, also distort the market's natural processes, by artificially inflating the price of labor. If the market is allowed to set these various rates, it is held that this will work ultimately for the prosperity of society. There is here a basic trust in the working of market forces and the feeling that in the economic sector, this is the best and safest way of regulating things. In this view, then, it would always, or almost always, be oxymoronic to speak of guiding or orienting the market toward the common good, since by definition, the market always tends toward the good of the whole.

To this point of view the Magisterium of the Catholic Church is definitely opposed. Before looking at the teaching of *Centesimus Annus*, I will discuss a few important instances that demonstrate the Church's consistent and long-standing opposition. In *Rerum Novarum*, Leo XIII stated that a man's work has to be regarded from two points of view, personal and necessary. Insofar as his work is personal, he has the right to work for any wages or for none at all (e.g., as a volunteer); but insofar as his work is necessary for his livelihood, he "has a right to procure what is required in order to live" (no. 44). Then Leo makes a statement that strikes at the very heart of the free market position: "There is a dictate of nature more imperious and more ancient than any bargain between man and man, that the remuneration must be enough to support the wage-earner in reasonable and frugal comfort" (ibid.). He goes on to say that if a worker is forced to accept less than a living wage, "he is the victim of force and injustice" (no. 45). These statements fly in the face of the idea, upheld by proponents of a free market, that market forces are the best way to arrive at wage justice.[7] Leo XIII thought otherwise, and his teaching has been repeated down to the present and figures prominently in *Centesimus*, as we will see.

The second instance of earlier Catholic social teaching is a striking quotation from Pius XI in *Quadragesimo Anno* (1931):

> Just as the unity of human society cannot be built upon "class" conflict, so the proper ordering of economic affairs cannot be left to the free play of rugged competition. From this source, as from a polluted spring, have proceeded all the errors of the "individualistic" school. This school, forgetful or ignorant of the social and moral aspects of economic activities, regarded these as completely free and immune from any intervention by public authority, for they would have in the market place and in unregulated competition a principle of self-direction more suitable for guiding them than any created intellect which might intervene. Free competition, however, though justified and quite useful within certain limits, cannot be an adequate controlling principle in economic affairs. This has been abundantly proved by the consequences that have followed from the free rein given to these dangerous individualistic ideas. (no. 88)

In this same encyclical Pius XI states that the economic proposals of the moderate socialists of his day "often strikingly approach the just demands of Christian social reformers" (no. 113).

So it is obvious that the tradition of papal social teaching from Leo XIII on did not accept the logic of the free market. Our question is: Does *Centesimus Annus* introduce new teaching here? Does it (in the words of Craycraft) "explicitly endorse the free market as the 'victorious social system' in the world, and as the type of economy that ought to be proposed in all places"?[8] I think we will see that it does not.

---

7 To show that I am not setting up a straw man, let me quote from an article by Fr. Robert Sirico. Commenting on Leo XIII and *Rerum Novarum*, he says: "It is apparent that he fails fully to grasp the manner in which wage rates affect the whole of the economy." And: "It is unfortunate that Leo didn't make the connection between the market wage and pricing system as the economically most efficient way to insure a living wage for workers." Robert Sirico, "Catholicism's Developing Social Teaching," *C. S. Lewis Society of California* (website), available at http://www.lewissociety. org/teaching.php as of August 2017. (Originally published in *The Freeman*, December 1991.)

8 "'Having' and 'Being': John Paul II as Pastor," in *A New Worldly Order*, 71.

In the first place, *Centesimus Annus* upholds the doctrine of the just wage taught by Leo XIII, Pius XI, Pius XII, and other popes.

> Society and the State must ensure wage levels adequate for the main-tenance of the worker and his family, including a certain amount for savings. (no. 15)

This in itself is a clear rejection of free market principles and effectively ought to end the argument. But *Centesimus* has much more to say about the market. Indeed, John Paul devotes more space to a discussion of the market mechanism than occurs in any previous encyclical. Does he see the market as essentially self-regulating or as something that needs to be subjected to intelligent control, a control that goes beyond market forces? By looking at a series of quotations from the encyclical, we will be able to answer this question.

After discussing a just society, John Paul II states:

> Such a society is not directed against the market, but demands that the market be appropriately controlled by the forces of society and by the State, so as to guarantee that the basic needs of the whole of society are satisfied. (no. 35)

Then a little later, the Holy Father writes:

> It is the task of the State to provide for the defense and preservation of common goods such as the natural and human environments, which cannot be safeguarded simply by market forces. (no. 40)

And in the same section:

> Here we find a new limit on the market: there are collective and qual-itative needs which cannot be satisfied by market mechanisms. There are important human needs which escape its logic. There are goods which by their very nature cannot and must not be bought or sold. Certainly the mechanisms of the market offer secure advantages.... Nevertheless, these mechanisms carry the risk of an "idolatry" of the market, an idolatry which ignores the existence of goods which by their nature are not and cannot be mere commodities. (no. 40)

I think that these three quotations make it very clear that John Paul does not accept the basic premise or logic of the free market, namely, that the market is essentially a self-regulating system that does not need deliberate human intervention to correct its outcomes. On the contrary, he is clear that the market needs to be controlled, that the market cannot be trusted to safeguard certain necessary goods.

Next let us look at one of the most important passages in the encyclical—one of the handful that those who interpret *Centesimus* as an endorsement of the free market rely on:

> Returning now to the initial question: can it perhaps be said that, after the failure of Communism, capitalism is the victorious social system, and that capitalism should be the goal of the countries now making efforts to rebuild their economy and society? Is this the model which ought to be proposed to the countries of the Third World which are searching for the paths to true economic and civil progress?
>
> The answer is obviously complex. If by "capitalism" is meant an economic system which recognizes the fundamental and positive role of business, the market, private property and the resulting responsibility for the means of production, as well as free human creativity in the economic sector, then the answer is certainly in the affirmative, even though it would perhaps be more appropriate to speak of a "business economy," "market economy" or simply "free economy." But if by "capitalism" is meant a system in which freedom in the economic sector is not circumscribed within a strong juridical framework which places it at the service of human freedom in its totality and sees it as a particular aspect of that freedom, the core of which is ethical and religious, then the reply is certainly negative. (no. 42)

What I think should be noted about this passage is that whatever *name* is given to a just social system, the content of that system—not its name—is what is important. And here again the pope calls for a "strong juridical framework" (that is, a legal framework) to orient the economy toward the total good of mankind. Thus this passage cannot be seen as an endorsement of the free market as that term is usually understood, and it is an endorsement of capitalism only if one pays close attention to what the pope means by this term. Moreover, in the very next paragraph, John

Paul, in commenting on the "multitudes...still living in conditions of great material and moral poverty," writes:

> There is a risk that a radical capitalistic ideology could spread which refuses even to consider these problems, in the *a priori* belief that any attempt to solve them is doomed to failure, and which blindly entrusts their solution to the free development of market forces. (no. 42)

John Paul II also includes in *Centesimus* comments on the existing capitalist economies of the Western world. These comments are important for our effort to understand the encyclical's teaching on the free market.

> The Western countries...run the risk of seeing [the collapse of Communism] as a one-sided victory of their own economic system, and thereby failing to make necessary corrections in that system. (no. 56)

And in his discussion of various responses of Western nations to communism after World War II, the Holy Father writes:

> Another kind of response, practical in nature, is represented by the affluent society or the consumer society. It seeks to defeat Marxism on the level of pure materialism by showing how a free-market society can achieve a greater satisfaction of material human needs than Communism, while equally excluding spiritual values. In reality, while on the one hand it is true that this social model shows the failure of Marxism to contribute to a humane and better society, on the other hand, insofar as it denies an autonomous existence and value to morality, law, culture and religion, it agrees with Marxism, in the sense that it totally reduces man to the sphere of economics and the satisfaction of material needs. (no. 19)

This is John Paul II's evaluation of the actual operation of free-market economies.

To be fair to *Centesimus* and to my readers, I will now discuss the principal passages in the encyclical that some have held to constitute an embrace of the free market. We have already seen one of these passages. Let us look briefly at the chief remaining ones and see to what extent they demand or allow such an interpretation.

It would appear that, on the level of individual nations and of international relations, *the free market* is the most efficient instrument for utilizing resources and effectively responding to needs. But this is true only for those needs which are "solvent," insofar as they are endowed with purchasing power, and for those resources which are "marketable," insofar as they are capable of obtaining a satisfactory price. But there are many human needs which find no place on the market. It is a strict duty of justice and truth not to allow fundamental human needs to remain unsatisfied, and not to allow those burdened by such needs to perish. (no. 34)

One can see that what appears to be an unqualified acceptance of the free market is immediately qualified and limited.

Another passage is as follows: "The modern *business economy* has positive aspects. Its basis is human freedom exercised in the economic field, just as it is exercised in many other fields" (no. 32). Few would deny these words of the pontiff, but they are hardly revolutionary in the context of Catholic social teaching. Modern business economies do have positive aspects, but to acknowledge this hardly constitutes an embrace of free market economics.

A little later, after a discussion of attacks on family life and children, John Paul says:

These criticisms are directed not so much against an economic system as against an ethical and cultural system. The economy in fact is only one aspect and one dimension of the whole of human activity. If economic life is absolutized, if the production and consumption of goods become the center of social life and society's only value, not subject to any other value, the reason is to be found not so much in the economic system itself as in the fact that the entire socio-cultural system, by ignoring the ethical and religious dimension, has been weakened, and ends by limiting itself to the production of goods and services alone. (no. 39)

And a bit later he states:

The Church respects *the legitimate autonomy of the democratic order.…*
    These general observations also apply to the *role of the State in the economic sector.* Economic activity, especially the activity of a

market economy, cannot be conducted in an institutional, juridical or political vacuum. On the contrary, it presupposes sure guarantees of individual freedom and private property, as well as a stable currency and efficient public services. Hence the principal task of the State is to guarantee this security, so that those who work and produce can enjoy the fruits of their labors and thus feel encouraged to work efficiently and honestly. (nos. 47 and 48)

These last two passages are probably the most difficult to harmonize in an entirely satisfactory way with the predominant message of *Centesimus*. But as I said earlier, we must take the encyclical as a whole, looking at its overall teaching and not pressing too far any one part, especially if it seems to contradict other parts of the encyclical or previous papal doctrine.

One of the most important yet difficult to understand themes in *Centesimus Annus* is freedom. To Americans, freedom is usually understood as absence of restraint, as each person's right to pursue happiness according to his own understanding and inclinations, so long as the rights of others are not affected. But this is not what John Paul means by freedom. In *Centesimus* he writes: "Freedom attains its full development only by accepting the truth" (no. 46). Unlike the notion of freedom as being able to do whatever one wants so long as others are not disturbed, John Paul II constantly links freedom with truth. He says of religious freedom that it is "the right to live in the truth of one's faith and in conformity with one's transcendent dignity as a person" (no. 47). In the long passage I quoted about whether capitalism should be considered as the "victorious social system" (no. 42), the Holy Father says that "freedom in the economic sector [must] be circumscribed within a strong juridical framework which places it at the service of human freedom in its totality...." I think this difficult concept must be understood as meaning that whenever anything external to the human person (whether economic forces, totalitarian political regimes, or anything at all) distorts man, man's freedom is thereby distorted. It is not because men cannot do whatever they want, but because our human nature is attacked that our true freedom is limited. But "human freedom in its totality" is not limited by government intervention into market processes, any more than the true freedom of automobile drivers is limited by stop signs and traffic lights.[9]

---

9 Other passages dealing with freedom are in nos. 36, 39, and 42.

Another point I think should always be borne in mind is that life in Communist Poland is the constant backdrop for this encyclical. John Paul alludes more than once to the breakdown in responsibility, the work ethic, and basic public trust that communism caused.[10] In calling for the creation of these virtues and in criticizing Communist economies, he is not calling for the free market as we understand it in the United States, but reacting against the heavy hand of Communist central planning and bureaucracy.

John Paul clearly condemns the Communist order, what he calls "real socialism." But in contrast to this, what kind of economic order is the Church promoting? Is the Church recommending any economic system? The following passage is relevant here.

> The Church has no models to present; models that are real and truly effective can only arise within the framework of different historical situations, through the efforts of all those who responsibly confront concrete problems in all their social, economic, political and cultural aspects, as these interact with one another. For such a task the Church offers her social teaching as an *indispensable and ideal orientation*, a teaching which, as already mentioned, recognizes the positive value of the market and of enterprise, but which at the same time points out that these need to be oriented towards the common good. (no. 43)

This is an interesting passage. Some, looking (it seems) only at the first clause of the first sentence, have claimed that the Church is saying that capitalism is the only game in town.

> With *Centesimus Annus*, Catholic social doctrine abandoned any quest for a "third way" between or beyond capitalism and socialism.[11]

But I do not think that is what *Centesimus Annus* is saying. Rather, it is reacting to the efforts of some Catholics in the 1930s and thereafter, following Pius XI's encyclical *Quadragesimo Anno*, to sketch out on paper rather grandiose *a priori* models for third way economic systems that were neither socialist nor capitalist.[12] What John Paul is saying, and indeed

---

10 See, e.g., nos. 24, 41, 47 and 48.

11 George Weigel, *Witness to Hope: the Biography of Pope John Paul II* (New York: Cliff Street Books, 1999), 615.

12 For example, see the detailed plans for industry councils on pages 6 and 7 of Mary Lois

what Pius XI himself was saying, is that this is the wrong way to proceed. Models cannot be created *a priori*, they must arise "within the framework of different historical situations." After all, in the Middle Ages, no philosopher or theologian sat down and sketched out an economic system based on the craft guilds. This quintessential Catholic approach to the economy arose from people struggling to apply Catholic moral principles to the actual contemporary economic situation.

Relevant to this also is the following neglected passage in *Centesimus*, which makes clear that John Paul has not decided that the capitalist option is all there is: "We have seen that it is unacceptable to say that the defeat of so-called 'Real Socialism' leaves capitalism as the only model of economic organization" (no. 35).[13] In fact, if any actual existing economy receives praise in *Centesimus Annus*, it is West Germany's "social market economy."[14]

Thus I think that, taken as a whole, the numerous qualifications put on the functioning of the market by John Paul II in *Centesimus* indicate clearly enough that he does not accept the logic of the free market. In this encyclical John Paul attempted to give guidance to the regnant capitalism of our time, much as Pius XI had sought to give friendly criticism and advice for Italy's Fascist economy in *Quadragesimo Anno*.[15] Catholic social teaching indeed is adapted to each age, but it is adapted from a core set of principles, principles that, because they are drawn from the nature of man and of society, are not changeable. The very different philosophical foundations that underlie free market economics and Catholic social teaching necessarily preclude the latter's embrace of the former. So whatever the future may hold for our society, papal teaching on the economy will continue to flow from the same basic principles as articulated by Leo XIII, Pius XI and John Paul II, until, at the end of time, Our Lord returns as our judge and savior.

Eberdt and Gerald J. Schnepp, *Industrialism and the Popes* (New York: P. J. Kenedy, 1953).

13 In the condensed version of *Centesimus* contained in *A New Worldly Order* and which originally appeared in *First Things* (August–September 1991), this passage is distorted and the word "capitalism" is rendered by the phrase in brackets as "[the present operation of capitalism]" (46).

14 In my discussion of *Centesimus* in chapter five I quoted St. John Paul's criticism of what he calls "the affluent society or the consumer society" (no. 19) as a response to communism after World War II. But immediately before that passage he had spoken of what he termed "a positive effort to rebuild a democratic society inspired by social justice..." (no. 19). He seems to be describing here West Germany's post-World War II economic system.

15 See nos. 91–95.

APPENDIX III

Review of *Compendium of the Social Doctrine of the Church*

ALTHOUGH STRICTLY SPEAKING NOT ITSELF A PART OF Catholic magisterial teaching on the social order, the *Compendium of the Social Doctrine of the Church* (2005) attempts to collect and summarize the Church's social doctrine. The following review was published in *New Oxford Review*, July/August 2006.

PONTIFICAL COUNCIL FOR JUSTICE AND PEACE, *COMPENDIUM OF THE SOCIAL DOCTRINE OF THE CHURCH*

(Washington: United States Conference of Catholic Bishops, 2005)

THE *COMPENDIUM OF THE SOCIAL DOCTRINE OF THE CHURCH*, LIKE any other work having any kind of doctrinal status, is not a book that can be reviewed exactly like other works. It is not simply the expression of an author's opinions, however well argued and however much based on a long intellectual tradition. Nor, however, in this case, is it simply a doctrinal statement of the Church. Rather, as is stated in no. 8, it is a compilation taken from "documents of differing authority. Alongside council documents and encyclicals there are also papal addresses and documents drafted by offices of the Holy See [so that]...the reader should be aware that different levels of teaching authority are involved." Moreover, since the *Compendium* was compiled by the Pontifical Council for Justice and Peace, which is itself simply an office of the Holy See, the selection and arrangement of the texts chosen would seem to lack any authority. So, for example, if some passages with true magisterial authority were placed under certain topics, there may be other documents possessing equal or even greater magisterial authority that the Council either excluded or placed under a different heading. The work becomes, then, a useful handbook of Catholic social doctrine, but no substitute for the original documents of the Magisterium. We should thus be careful about basing any substantial argument on social matters solely on the *Compendium* itself. We must still try to understand the rich corpus of Catholic social doctrine in its context and entirety by reading and consulting the original documents.

But the *Compendium* does have several useful purposes. First, it is a suggestive guide to the incredible wealth of papal and other statements on social matters that it quotes and references. Whenever a large volume of material is produced, intelligent access to that material soon becomes a problem, and thus the need for guides, indexes, and the like. This is certainly true of the doctrinal patrimony of the Church as a whole, but it is also true of her social teaching. There are not only encyclicals, but also numerous papal addresses and letters, not to mention the documents issued by various Roman congregations. Although the *Compendium* is hardly an exhaustive list, it does contain many references to documents, both well-known and obscure, which even serious students of the subject might overlook. So if useful for no other reason, the *Compendium* is a valuable guide to further reading.

But more than a compilation of texts, the *Compendium* is an integrated discussion of each topic it covers. Each of its twelve chapters treats a different topic — such as the human person, basic principles of the Church's social doctrine, the family, work, economic life, and politics. The numerous quotations from and citations to original documents are fully referenced and ground the discussion in the primary texts of the Catholic social heritage.

But what of the substance of the book's doctrinal presentation? As many readers know, in the last fifteen years or so a fierce battle has raged between those who claim that the Church has abandoned aspects of her patrimony of social doctrine and those who argue that, whatever change in terminology and emphasis may have occurred, the social teaching of the latter part of John Paul II's pontificate is solidly grounded in the tradition of his predecessors. This controversy centers on the 1991 encyclical *Centesimus Annus*, but has implications that are far wider. Indeed, it goes to the heart of the Catholic doctrine on the state and political authority, matters that were raised by Vatican II's decree on religious liberty. Let us see what the *Compendium* has to say on these topics.

Although political questions are relegated to chapter eight of this volume, logically they come before economic concerns, as both Leo XIII and Pius XI suggested. For the classical liberalism, as well as socialism, that these popes were fighting against (and that has been revived in our own time by such dissenters as Fr. Robert Sirico) is primarily a doctrine of the state and of the nature of society, which in turn has implications for economic activity. But its doctrine of the state is logically prior. Here the *Compendium* is clear, quoting John XXIII, and referring in a note to Leo XIII, that political authority, "no less than society itself, has its source in nature, and has, consequently, God for its author" (no. 393). The full consequences of this teaching are not drawn out here, but a reader who is willing to consult the "political" encyclicals of Leo XIII, such as *Immortale Dei* and *Libertas*, will find its implications discussed at length. Suffice it to say, if the state and its authority are from God, then a state is not only bound by the moral law in its political actions, just as individuals are, but the state cannot be simply a human creation that watches passively while men pursue their various egotistical activities, intervening only occasionally to keep the peace. It would have been well if Leo's encyclicals had been more fully referenced here, as well as the *Syllabus of Errors* by Blessed Pius IX. But for the discerning reader, the matter is clear.

Interestingly, the *Compendium* includes a section on the state and punishment which makes clear that the purpose of punishment is more than the mere restraint of a person in order to protect public safety. "Punishment does not serve merely the purpose of defending the public order and guaranteeing the safety of persons; it becomes as well an instrument for the correction of the offender, a correction that also takes on a moral value of expiation when the guilty party voluntarily accepts his punishment" (no. 403). This would seem to go clearly against the reigning view in the West today, which has absolutely no notion or understanding of "moral expiation."

Many people identify the Church's social doctrine exclusively with her teaching on economic morality. Though this is a mistake, nevertheless economic morality is an important part of her doctrinal patrimony. Here the *Compendium* has two chapters, six and seven (the first of which deals with work and the second with economic life), as well as important portions of chapter four (which presents the principles of the Church's social doctrine). Briefly, we can say that the *Compendium* upholds the teaching of the Church, expressed so many times, that economic life cannot be separated from ethical concerns. Thus the market, for example, however useful it may be for achieving purely material goals, is not its own regulator. As John Paul's encyclical *Centesimus Annus* said more than once, the free market must be explicitly regulated by man, including by the state. In fact, *Centesimus* is much more explicit about the need for state regulation of the economy than the *Compendium* is. But as soon as one admits the fact that the market is simply a tool, and must be judged by its results, then the entire foundation of classical liberal economics is overthrown. For according to classical liberal doctrine, the free market is its own judge, and, except perhaps for a few extreme cases, whatever it brings about is *ipso facto* socially good, at least in the long run. But Catholic doctrine can never accept such an opinion. To do so would be to overthrow not only common sense observation of the world and the insights of real economics, but also the constant teaching of the Magisterium of the Church. Unless development of doctrine can mean destruction of doctrine, the doctrines that the Church has long held and fostered cannot be jettisoned in a supposed papal change of heart.

Remarkably, the *Compendium* includes two separate paragraphs condemning usury (nos. 323 and 341). This in spite of the fact that everyone thinks he *knows* that the Church has "changed her teaching" on this subject. But we read: "Although the quest for equitable profit is acceptable in economic and financial activity, recourse to usury is to be morally condemned" (no. 341), and in the same paragraph, quoting the *Catechism*: "Those whose usurious and avaricious dealings lead to the hunger and death of their brethren...indirectly commit homicide, which is imputable to them." Usury between nations is also strongly rebuked, and the paragraph concludes by calling it (quoting John Paul II) "a scourge that is also a reality in our time and that has a stranglehold on many peoples' lives."

Although the encyclicals of such popes as Leo XIII and Pius XI on marriage are not always considered part of the Church's social patrimony, there is every reason why they should be seen as part of that doctrine in the wider sense. Even many parts of the Church's teaching on economic morality, such as the living wage, are rooted in her doctrine of the family. And in our time the question of the family has definitely come to the fore. This is because the satanic forces of disorder, which have destroyed so many of Christendom's unities — such as the unity between morality and politics and between morality and economics — have now begun to directly assault the family. Even in the nineteenth century this had begun with the spread of divorce, against which both Pius IX and Leo XIII protested. But today it is contraception, abortion, the absurdity of same-sex unions, and cloning, all of which directly attack man not only in his social relations, but in the very citadel of his personhood. Appropriately, the *Compendium* places the family among the first topics it considers (chapter five), highlighting especially the teaching of John Paul II, who taught so richly on this matter.

The *Compendium* also contains chapters dealing with human rights, international relations, and the environment. The chapter on war and peace is especially important today, when so many Catholics seem to replace the absolute demands of the Gospel with the reasons of state advanced by their governments. Important too is the quotation from John Paul at the end of the chapter on the environment, which demands the "adoption of new lifestyles...inspired by sobriety, temperance, and self-discipline.... There is a need to break with the logic of mere consumption and promote forms of agricultural and industrial production that respect the order of creation and satisfy the basic human needs of all" (no. 486). As Americans, residents of a nation that consumes a huge share of the earth's resources, well in excess of our percentage of the world's population, we should take such words to heart. St. Paul's warning about being content if we have food and clothing (I Timothy 6:8) seems especially relevant as we continue to acquire bigger cars and houses.

Because the material with which the *Compendium* deals is so diffuse, and because one must admit that the style of many recent papal and ecclesiastical documents has given rise to conflicting interpretations, I cannot stress enough the necessity of acquainting oneself with the fullness of the social tradition of the Catholic Church. The attempt to distill that tradition in the *Compendium*, while not without value as a reference, should not be confused with the tradition itself. There are too many documents left unmentioned, and much emphasis on only recent statements of the Holy See. But however much the *Compendium* does or does not fulfill its purpose, if anyone is moved to study and embrace the Church's social doctrine to any degree, the work will have achieved its aim. For since man is a social animal, the Church's social teaching cannot be regarded as something extra, something unnecessary, something which is a fad and perhaps a concession to left-wing concerns. No, for without this doctrine the Church must concede the social order to Satan and content herself with a personal piety and morality that ultimately will have as much to do with human life as do the ethical teachings of the mainstream Protestant denominations. Satan would like nothing better than to have his title as Prince of this World implicitly recognized by Catholics who are confused by the propaganda of dissent. But we cannot let that happen. Instead we must raise the banner of Jesus Christ the King, and proclaim him as king of nations and peoples, king of individuals, king of every aspect of human life. This is the ultimate aim of social doctrine and an aim that should be dear to every truly Catholic heart.

APPENDIX IV

Is Economic Justice Possible in this World?

I FIRST BECAME AWARE OF CATHOLIC SOCIAL TEACHING when I was in high school and read Richard Tawney's *Religion and the Rise of Capitalism*. Later I discovered the papal social encyclicals and the voluminous secondary literature of commentaries and studies. And later still I became sufficiently acquainted with it so that I began to talk to others and eventually to write about it. In the course of this I have noticed again and again the same reactions among that minority of Catholics who have at least heard of the Church's social doctrine. Confining myself to Catholics who profess to be orthodox and to conform their beliefs to the teaching of the Magisterium, there are, of course, some who wholeheartedly accept Catholic social teaching. But I am afraid that the larger number does not. Of these, one encounters, first, libertarians, or near libertarians — those who attribute to the free market some quasi-divine ability to sort out the rights and wrongs of human behavior and who oppose any, or almost any, interference with its workings. A few in this group make no bones about their contempt for and rejection of Catholic social teaching. Because it does not accord with their own ideas about wealth creation or competition or assorted other economic ideas, they regard the papal teaching — especially before *Centesimus Annus* — with open derision. Despite this, they manage to retain a reputation for orthodoxy.

The second and larger group is less forthright. Though as equally addicted to the same or similar propositions about wealth creation and competition as the first group, they are not so bold about their rejection of the Church's social teaching. Sometimes, by selective quotation or silence, they even attempt to make it seem as if the popes agreed with them. This group also maintains a reputation for orthodoxy.

Lastly, there is a group that claims to respect this teaching and to reject its contrary, but nevertheless its attitude toward the teaching is rather strange. For while professing a regard for it, these people maintain — sometimes openly, sometimes by implication — that Catholic social teaching is too unworldly, impractical, altogether impossible to implement in this life. It is with this last group that I am chiefly concerned here. And although I do not agree with this group, I will concede one point to them, namely, that it is very difficult to bring about any kind of just social order.

Reasons to doubt the feasibility of really implementing Catholic social teaching are easy to understand. Aside from the initial problem of persuading the majority, especially those in positions of power, that social justice according to the Church's vision is something to strive for, the logistical problem of making a transition from what we have now to what we desire is overwhelming. The economy is not something that exists just on paper. The decisions that have been made in the past have created an entire network of economic and legal relationships and an infrastructure of factories, means of transportation, centers of population, and so on. Gigantic sums of money have been invested in certain ways, and the owners of those sums are not likely to meekly accept any diminution of their profits or power. And, for example, if we decided that one of the things we wanted to do was to foster the family farm, we would have to deal with the fact that such farms are declining in number, their owners are aging, and there are fewer younger people trained and interested in farming. Moreover, because of the complexity and interrelatedness of the economy, as soon as you begin to deal with one sector another sector becomes involved. Banking and credit, for example, touch all the other sectors intimately. Production involves transportation and questions of tariffs and trade agreements. And since worldwide trade agreements have been negotiated and signed, one country could only with difficulty institute policies radically at variance with the rest of the world. Altogether it seems like an impossible task.

But I would like to compare the difficulty of the task with the difficulties involved in another area of Catholic morality: chastity. Is it feasible to expect the world to become chaste? Here the problems seem at least as daunting. In our own country and in most of the West, we have not just indifference to chastity, but outright hostility. Many are convinced that chastity is not just impossible, but psychologically unhealthy, an example of cultural repression, the unfortunate legacy of the "pale Galilean," from whose breath "the world has grown gray."[1] Governments, international organizations, and much of big business are actively working against chastity; it is only pregnancy they disapprove of, not sexual activity, no matter how unchaste or bizarre. Added to this, of course, is the fact that even for those of the human race firmly committed to the preservation of chastity, it is a constant struggle simply to keep oneself and one's children chaste. Without doubt it is a difficult virtue.

All this and more is true, yet one rarely finds those who are full of doubts about the feasibility of doing anything about Catholic social teaching taking the same view on chastity. Suggest to them that perhaps we should accommodate ourselves to the frailties of human nature, and we are immediately and loudly denounced as modernists, traitors to the faith, worldlings. Nor do I disagree with that diagnosis. I am as committed as anyone to preaching chastity and doing everything possible to uphold it. All I ask is that we extend the same courtesy to this other and equally important area of Christian morals, the social doctrine of the Church. It would seem to me that, whatever obstacles there are to implementing Catholic social teaching, the obstacles to achieving worldwide chastity are just as great. But in neither case are these obstacles a sufficient cause for us to abandon the struggle.

There is moreover a special reason for regarding the social doctrine of the Church as something we should actually seek to implement. A specific condemnation has been reserved for those who belittle it, including those who merely give it lip service. Pius XI wrote in his first encyclical, *Ubi Arcano* (December 23, 1922), about the great number of those

> who profess Catholic teaching...concerning the rights and duties of laborers on land or in industry...and yet by their spoken and written word, and the whole tenor of their lives, act as if the teaching and oft-repeated precepts of the Sovereign Pontiffs...had lost their efficacy or were completely out of date. In all this we recognize a kind of moral, judicial, and social Modernism, and We condemn it as strongly as We do dogmatic Modernism. (nos. 60–61)

Orthodox Catholics rightly hate dogmatic modernism, and are rightly dismayed at its resurgence following the Second Vatican Council. But

---

1 "Thou hast conquered, O pale Galilean; the world has grown gray from thy breath." From Algernon Charles Swinburne (1837–1909), "Hymn to Proserpine."

ought we not equally to hate "moral, judicial, and social Modernism," and "condemn it as strongly as" the other? If our orthodoxy and loyalty to Catholic doctrine and to the Magisterium are genuine, then it should be evident in every area, not just where we find it convenient or where it fits in with our political opinions.

In some cases I fear that Catholics who deny the importance of this social teaching hold opinions more akin to those of some Lutheran thinkers — that this world is so utterly corrupted that it is not in any sense redeemable. According to this view, since man himself is radically corrupted, his institutions necessarily are also. Thus the most we can hope for is that individuals are saved; the social order had best be left to the Devil. But such a notion is entirely opposed to any Catholic conception of things. These words of Pius XI, from his encyclical *Quas Primas* (December 1925), give a striking picture of what the Church holds out as her ideal.

> If princes and magistrates duly elected are filled with the persuasion that they rule, not by their own right, but by the mandate and in place of the Divine King, they will exercise their authority piously and wisely, and they will make laws and administer them while having in view the common good and also the human dignity of their subjects. The result will be a stable peace and tranquility, for there will be no longer any cause for discontent. Men will see in their kings or in their rulers men like themselves, perhaps unworthy or open to criticism, but they will not on that account refuse obedience if they see reflected in them the authority of Christ, God and Man. Peace and harmony, too, will result, for with the spread and the universal extent of the Kingdom of Christ men will become more and more conscious of the link that binds them together, and thus many conflicts will be either prevented entirely, or at least their bitterness will be diminished. (no. 19)

Pius XI sees here a social and political order that is permeated with the spirit of Jesus Christ. Far from being necessarily alienated from him, those who hold political power are expected to rule "in place of the Divine King."

The serious difficulties that exist, then, are not good reasons for Catholics to fail to embrace the social teachings. But there is one reason that almost seems to justify the hostility toward and lack of interest in doing something about the Church's social teachings. This is the need for an organized and coordinated approach to social questions. In the case of chastity, generally all that is required is an individual exercise of will, strengthened by divine grace. We are not dependent on others' decisions as to whether we will be chaste or not. But this is not true with regard to social justice. As I said, all aspects of the economy are interrelated. If a person has savings, what is he to do with them? Even if he simply places them in a savings account, how is he to know what the financial institution does with the money? Is it loaned out for a good or an evil purpose, at a just or unjust rate of interest? Individual businessmen are involved in a complicated system of prices, to a great extent beyond their control. And although much more could be done, especially by large corporations, to pay just wages right now, still the entire system of wages is larger than one company or entrepreneur. Each economic actor is not entirely his own master. Amintore Fanfani, in *Catholicism, Protestantism and Capitalism*, relates the following anecdote:

> I remember that in a little village in Tuscany there were only two bakeries. The owner of the one wished to close on Sunday, but was unable to do so because his rival kept open, and had he himself failed to follow suit he would have lost his customers who, being restaurant-keepers, wanted fresh bread on Sundays as well as week-days.[2]

The more complicated the economy, the more does such interdependence exist. In short, in social morality we often depend upon the decisions of other people, our individual responsibility is often less clear, and many times there are questions that involve that murky and less precise area of moral theology known as *cooperation*.

As a result, just as one nation could barely bring about economic justice for itself, it is hardly possible for one firm or one individual to do so. What is needed, then, is some kind of cooperation among economic actors. In 1931, in his encyclical *Quadragesimo Anno*, Pius XI had already called for such cooperation to solve the grave problems of society — cooperation between different employers, between employers and employees, and among the various nations. Now one would have to be a fool not to realize that to secure such cooperation would undoubtedly be extremely hard. But there is one thing that tends to make it even harder than it need be. And

2 *Catholicism, Protestantism and Capitalism* (New York: Sheed & Ward, 1939), 33.

unfortunately we are at present doing this one thing. What is that? It is to do nothing, not even to request such cooperation, not even to present it as an ideal. There are many problems in the world and in the Church today. And those that we recognize we generally work toward solving. We hold meetings and international conferences, write articles, sign treaties, pass laws. But to secure economic justice next to nothing is done. Of course it would be difficult. But all the problems of the world and the Church are difficult. If we do nothing we cannot expect even to begin to solve them. So to say that the problems of creating a just economy are impossible to solve, when we really do not even seriously desire to solve them, serves simply to justify our slothfulness.

Moreover, when we think about working toward a just social order, we should keep in mind the limitations of living in a fallen world. Cardinal Ratzinger wrote about *mishpat*, the Hebrew word for justice, in *A Turning Point for Europe?*:

> Reason and will must attempt to make concrete and to put into practice the criterion of God's *mishpat*, set up by faith, in changing historical situations, always in the essential imperfectability of man's action within history. It is not permitted to man to set up the "Kingdom," but he is charged to go toward the Kingdom through justice and love. The necessary mediation contained in the concept of *mishpat* indicates at the same time the precisely theological and methodological *locus* of Catholic (Christian) social doctrine. Faith's hope always goes infinitely farther than all our realizations, reaching into the realm of the eternal; but precisely the fact that this hope is given to us gives us the courage to take up again and again, despite all inadequacy, the struggle for a just order that is the form of freedom and builds up a dam against the tyranny of injustice.[3]

Just as in our work toward chastity, or any other virtue, so in our work toward social justice: we should be aware of "the essential imperfectability of man's action within history," but we are "charged to go toward the Kingdom through justice and love."[4] We will never reach that kingdom in this world and life, but that is not reason enough never to try.

But what concrete steps, if any, could we take to try to bring about

3 *A Turning Point for Europe?* (San Francisco: Ignatius, 1994), 77.
4 Ibid.

economic justice? Before answering this question, let me deal briefly with one more objection. In view of the many grave problems in the world today—the horrible reality of abortion, the probable impending legal acceptance of euthanasia, the attacks on family life, the defection of hundreds of thousands of Catholics from the Church—is now the time for us, for anyone, to work actively for the establishment of economic justice? I believe that it is, or rather, that it can be. I concede that abortion is certainly a graver issue, for it is a worse injustice to take someone's life than merely his job or his home. But everyone has a different vocation, and those who think that they are called to work in pursuit of justice in economic life ought not to be criticized by, nor to criticize, those who believe they are called to work to prevent the murder of the unborn or the aged or in some other area. There are many legitimate apostolates in Christ's Mystical Body.

Having said this, what is to be done? First, there is a great need for education, to simply spread the idea and desire for economic justice. So many have been warped in their thinking by capitalism that they do not realize the necessity of applying ethical criteria to economic activity. They do not understand that an economy has to be judged by how well it is performing its function. What is an economy's function? To provide the necessary and helpful material goods for the human race so that we can then in turn devote our energies to the more important matters—to our families and friends, to learning, to God. If an economy has instead fixed our attention on acquiring more and more (mostly useless) material goods, if it has disrupted settled communities by shifting about jobs for no good reason, if it has enabled some men to grow rich not by making useful goods but by manipulating money and monetary instruments, then that economy is a failure, despite the abundance of glittery things it has produced. We Americans tend to congratulate ourselves because the shelves in our stores are full. But this is not how to evaluate an economy. As St. John Paul II wrote in *Centesimus Annus*:

> It is therefore necessary to create lifestyles in which the quest for truth, beauty, goodness and communion with others for the sake of common growth are the factors which determine consumer choices, savings and investment. (no. 36)

I submit that in our economy this is far from being the case.

In the much-maligned days before the Second Vatican Council there existed among many Catholics a consciousness that there *was* something wrong with the economy, and that it must be reshaped in accordance with papal teaching. This consciousness was simply one sign of the relative health of the Catholic mind at the time; Catholics took the faith seriously, including the social apostolate. This being the case, actual schemes were created to bring about a greater degree of social justice. For example, labor schools and the Association of Catholic Trade Unionists tried to give people engaged in union activity an understanding of social doctrine. Fr. John Cronin wrote not only *Catholic Social Principles*, but also *Catholic Social Action*, which he termed "a guide and manual for social action." Hilaire Belloc's *The Restoration of Property* suggested actual legislative proposals to bring about a society with a more just distribution of property. Despite the collapse of Catholic life and loyalty since the 1960s, some of this type of work can still be done. There is room for such worthy projects as organizing labor unions for low-paid service workers or forming credit unions in rural or poor urban areas. There is even room for a vocation as a legislator, although such an occupation is extremely dangerous to the soul, considering the many temptations from intellectual and moral sellouts that Catholics in politics face today. But until more Catholics have absorbed the entire vision of the Church's teaching on social justice, I am not sanguine that these efforts will bring about a reform of the economy as a whole. Since the Church is presently so distracted with questions that concern the very foundations of the faith, most Catholics do not have the time to absorb this vision of a just society. But since social doctrine is an integral part of the Gospel, any attempt to restore the Catholic mind, to restore discipline in the Church, must include a due emphasis on social justice. If this is done, if we begin to think as Catholics in every department of our lives, then there may be scope for more than ad hoc projects. Until that time, we must study social doctrine, absorb it, and teach it to others. In this way we will be doing much to restore the Catholic mind, as well as making the necessary preparations to establish a just economy. It is nearly all we can do now, but it is a large and worthy project.

EPILOGUE

Catholic Social Teaching: Homage to Christ the King

IN THE PASSAGE FROM POPE PIUS XI'S ENCYCLICAL *UBI Arcano* that I have already quoted in this book, the pontiff speaks of "Catholic teaching concerning social authority and the due regard for it, concerning the rights and duties of laborers on land or in industry,... and finally the rights of the Creator, Redeemer, and Lord, Christ Himself, over men and nations..." (no. 60). Even if we are well disposed toward Catholic social teaching, we are not likely to link "Catholic teaching... concerning the rights and duties of laborers on land or in industry" with "the rights of the Creator, Redeemer, and Lord, Christ Himself, over men and nations." Why is that? I think it is because we have lost the habit, and often even the concept, of a hierarchical way of thinking. After all, economics and theology are taught in different academic departments; neither businessmen nor economists take many of their cues from religion. And it is rare to hear any homilist mention the Church's authoritative teaching on "the rights and duties of laborers on land or in industry." So they seem like two different things, or at best two unrelated parts of Church teaching.

No faithful Catholic would deny that Jesus Christ should be king over each person's heart, in fact, over every member of the human race. But men are not just individual creatures. We form families, villages, nations, as well as many other bodies including corporations, cooperatives, societies, clubs, and the like. Should Jesus Christ be ruler over all these too? Should their fundamental laws, constitutions, or articles of agreement reflect in some way the kingship of Christ? And if it is wrong for an individual to do something, is it likewise wrong for an institution to do the same thing, even if that institution is a corporation or a government?

A few years after his first encyclical, Pope Pius answered such questions in *Quas Primas* (1925), an encyclical that deals explicitly with the kingship of Jesus Christ. His statement of the extent of Christ's rule is striking: "Nor is there any difference in this matter between the individual and the family or the state; for all men, whether collectively or individually, are under the dominion of Christ" (no. 18). The entire encyclical is devoted to explaining the meaning of the "dominion of Christ," and Pope Pius took advantage of this occasion to institute the Feast of Christ the King in the liturgy for the first time.

So what does this far-reaching kingship of Christ mean? What in particular does it mean for Catholic social teaching? If all men are subject to Jesus Christ, both as individuals and in all their social and political associations, then those social and political associations are bound by the law of Christ equally with individuals. Obviously that precludes governments from approving such abominations as abortion or same-sex unions. But it goes much further than that. If I as an individual am not permitted to mislead or cajole my neighbor into buying something from me by taking advantage of his weakness, need, or stupidity, then neither are corporations or other business firms permitted to do so. But is not much advertising simply an appeal to the weakest parts of human nature in the attempt to persuade us to buy things we most likely do not need? If I as an individual am not permitted to callously make use of my neighbors for years and then turn my back on them with contempt, then neither are corporations permitted to do so. But most corporations will make use of the governmental, communal, and social infrastructure, both material and non-material, and then blithely pull up stakes and head for some place where they can make a greater profit, perhaps leaving behind a town that has now lost its main source of jobs and income. Of course I do not deny the necessity for a firm to make a profit, in the sense of taking in enough to cover all expenses, including just payments to shareholders. But as Pope Benedict reminded us in his encyclical *Caritas in Veritate*:

> business management cannot concern itself only with the interests of the proprietors, but must also assume responsibility for all the other stakeholders who contribute to the life of the business: the workers, the clients, the suppliers of various elements of production, the community of reference. (no. 40)

If a company has prospered in part because of faithful and hardworking employees, loyal local customers or suppliers, and a benevolent attitude on the part of the municipal and state authorities, then it is not asking too much for their needs and interests to be taken into account in business decisions. This is part of what I called the hierarchical relationship between economic activity and the rest of human life. Economic activity is for the sake of fulfilling human needs and supporting human life. It is not an end in itself. Profit is not an end in itself, but is useful only if it is a sign that the firm is supplying some human need and playing its part in the great hierarchy of human actions that reaches from our lowest activities up to Jesus Christ, king of creation. Pope Pius XI himself expressed it as follows:

> For it is the moral law alone which commands us to seek in all our conduct our supreme and final end, and to strive directly in our specific actions for those ends which nature, or rather the Author of nature, has established for them, duly subordinating the particular to the general. If this law be faithfully obeyed, the result will be that particular economic aims, whether of society as a body or of individuals, will be intimately linked with the universal teleological order, and as a consequence we shall be led by progressive stages to the final end of all, God Himself, our highest and lasting good. (*Quadragesimo Anno*, no. 43)

Whether it be the state, a religious order, or a sports club, every type of human association has its own peculiar purpose. Obviously, the constitution and rules of a religious order and a sports club will be very different. One will attempt to serve God and further the cause of the Church directly, the other will attempt to promote some sporting activity directly. But although the latter does not *directly* aim at the glory of God the way a religious community does, it is nonetheless part of the hierarchy of human activity, that "universal teleological order," which leads to God. If a team schedules its games or practices so that its members have no time for Sunday Mass, then it has clearly placed itself in opposition to God and his laws. If it adopts the policy of having cheerleaders who are an occasion of sin because of their scanty clothing, here also it offends against the law of God. If it fosters such a spirit of partisanship that supporters of rival teams are treated with contempt or even violence, there also it disregards and violates the commandments of God. Or even if a team demands so much that its members have insufficient time for family life, then that team is demanding more than it has a right to. The point is that while a sports team rightly intends to promote sport as its primary mission, it must recognize that there are higher aims than sport. If another team practices every Sunday morning and thereby wins more games, that team has attempted to elevate sports and winning as independent goals totally divorced from God, no longer a part of the hierarchy of creation offering homage to Christ the King. But our team, of course, has no right to increase its practices at the expense of our religious duties or our family life even if its rivals have done so.

Everything, every activity, in its own way must give praise to God and at the same time help human beings to attain Heaven. Sports can do this when they provide necessary and healthy recreation. But the minute a sport is seen as an end in itself, it is no longer part of the great hierarchy of human acts that nourish and help us toward eternal life. Similarly, when economic activity provides the external goods and services mankind needs in order to live, at the same time providing a decent living for all involved in the productive process, then economic activity is part of that hierarchy of means and ends leading up to God, part of the homage to Christ the King that mankind is bound to offer. But as soon as businesses see profit, or even production, as ends in themselves, divorced from the larger human picture, then they are no longer contributing toward the ultimate end of human life but are actually leading us away from God. For as the Second Vatican Council taught, Catholics must "labor vigorously so that men may become capable of constructing the temporal order rightly and directing it to God through Christ" (*Decree on the Apostolate of the Laity*, no. 7).

There is nothing wrong with enjoying the many activities that God provides for us in this life. Indeed, Sacred Scripture contains celebrations of many ordinary human acts, including sexual love and drinking wine. But as soon as these or any other human activity lead us away from our attainment of eternal life, then they become a sin, and no longer fit into the grand symphony of man's activities that can glorify God.

If we go on a family vacation to the beach, there is nothing wrong in enjoying our stops along the way, either our stops for food or our stays in motels. It is perfectly all right to enjoy our time in the motel swimming pool. But suppose we enjoy a certain motel so much that we forget about the beach and never get there at all. That would allow something that is supposed to contribute toward our final goal to become the final goal itself. Of course, there is nothing wrong with changing vacation plans. But we do not have that same freedom with our human destiny. Like it or not, we are headed toward that final meeting with Jesus Christ. As the Epistle to the Hebrews in the New Testament puts it: "It is appointed unto man once to die, and after that the judgment" (9:27). So while we must engage in many different activities in this world, and many of them we can enjoy, we cannot let any of them rob us of our final goal, eternal life with Jesus Christ.

Now if all this is true, then it applies to men whether as individuals or as groups. It is true that human beings are saved or damned as individuals. But as I pointed out already, we cannot ignore God's law just because we are acting as part of a group. Pope Pius XI noted that our economic actions, "whether of society as a body or of individuals," must be linked to that hierarchy that has God as its apex. Catholics especially should try to make sure that the very structures of our communal and corporate organizations, from the state to the family and everything in between, will not hinder—and if possible will even promote—the glory of God and the salvation of mankind. The larger and more complex an organization is, the more we must take care that it does not begin to exist for itself alone, free from the rule of Jesus Christ. Many of the social encyclicals since Leo XIII devote much space to topics such as relations between employers and employees, between one industry and another, and between international trading partners—because the supreme pontiffs have always known that it is easy for sin to enter into human affairs. Particularly in the modern world, we experience not just simple human sin any more, but what John Paul II called "structures of sin"—institutions and established patterns of behavior that embody, promote, and continue sin. As much as possible, we should try to set up "structures of virtue" instead. Only in that way will the kingship that Jesus Christ holds over the human race be manifested in our conduct and in the conduct of nations and of all the institutions and associations that we use and enjoy in our pilgrimage to our true and eternal Fatherland.

ABOUT THE AUTHOR

THOMAS STORCK WRITES WIDELY ON THE subjects of Catholic social teaching and Catholic culture and history. He is the author of four previous books and of numerous articles in periodicals and online. He is a contributing editor of *The Distributist Review* and a member of the editorial board of *The Chesterton Review*.